ARBITRARY BORDERS

Political Boundaries in World History

South America

NICARAGUA
PANAMA
COSTA RICA
EL SALVADOR

GRENADA
BARBADOS
TRINIDAD AND TOBAGO
VENEZUELA
GUYANA
SURINAME
French Guiana
(FRANCE)

COLOMBIA

ECUADOR

Galapagos Is.
(ECUADOR)

PERU

BRAZIL

BOLIVIA

*PACIFIC
OCEAN*

PARAGUAY

*ATLANTIC
OCEAN*

CHILE

URUGUAY

ARGENTINA

N

0   800 miles
0   800 km

Falkland Is.
(UNITED KINGDOM)

© Infobase Publishing

ARBITRARY BORDERS

Political Boundaries in World History

A South American Frontier:
The Tri-Border Region

Daniel K. Lewis
California State
Polytechnic University, Pomona

Foreword by
Senator **George J. Mitchell**

Introduction by
James I. Matray
California State University, Chico

CHELSEA HOUSE
P U B L I S H E R S
An imprint of Infobase Publishing

FRONTIS The tri-border region is located in east-central South America, where the countries of Argentina, Brazil, and Paraguay meet.

A South American Frontier: The Tri-Border Region

Copyright © 2006 by Infobase Publishing

Chelsea House
An imprint of Infobase Publishing
132 West 31st Street
New York NY 10001

Library of Congress Cataloging-in-Publication Data

Lewis, Daniel K., 1959-
  A South American frontier : the Tri-Border Region / Daniel Lewis.
  p. cm. — (Arbitrary borders)
  Includes bibliographical references and index.
  ISBN 0-7910-8649-6 (hardcover)
  1. Tri-Border Area (Argentina, Brazil and Paraguay)—History. I. Title. II. Series.
  F2217.L49 2006
  981'.62—dc22   2005036020

Chelsea House books are available at special discounts when purchased in bulk quantities for businesses, associations, institutions, or sales promotions. Please call our Special Sales Department in New York at (212) 967–8800 or (800) 322–8755.

You can find Chelsea House on the World Wide Web at
http://www.chelseahouse.com

Text and cover design by Keith Trego

Printed in the United States of America

Bang EJB 10 9 8 7 6 5 4 3 2 1

This book is printed on acid-free paper.

All links and web addresses were checked and verified to be correct at the time of publication. Because of the dynamic nature of the web, some addresses and links may have changed since publication and may no longer be valid.

Contents

Foreword

Senator **George J. Mitchell**

I spent years working for peace in Northern Ireland and in the Middle East. I also made many visits to the Balkans during the long and violent conflict there.

Each of the three areas is unique; so is each conflict. But there are also some similarities: in each, there are differences over religion, national identity, and territory.

Deep religious differences that lead to murderous hostility are common in human history. Competing aspirations involving national identity are more recent occurrences, but often have been just as deadly.

Territorial disputes—two or more people claiming the same land—are as old as humankind. Almost without exception, such disputes have been a factor in recent conflicts. It is impossible to calculate the extent to which the demand for land—as opposed to religion, national identity, or other factors—figures in the motivation of people caught up in conflict. In my experience it is a substantial factor that has played a role in each of the three conflicts mentioned above.

In Northern Ireland and the Middle East, the location of the border was a major factor in igniting and sustaining the conflict. And it is memorialized in a dramatic and visible way: through the construction of large walls whose purpose is to physically separate the two communities.

In Belfast, the capital and largest city in Northern Ireland, the so-called "Peace Line" cuts through the heart of the city, right across urban streets. Up to thirty feet high in places, topped with barbed wire in others, it is an ugly reminder of the duration and intensity of the conflict.

In the Middle East, as I write these words, the government of Israel has embarked on a huge and controversial effort to construct a security fence roughly along the line that separates Israel from the West Bank.

Having served a tour of duty with the U.S. Army in Berlin, which was once the site of the best known of modern walls, I am skeptical of their long-term value, although they often serve short-term needs. But it cannot be said that such structures represent a new idea. Ancient China built the Great Wall to deter nomadic Mongol tribes from attacking its population.

In much the same way, other early societies established boundaries and fortified them militarily to achieve the goal of self-protection. Borders always have separated people. Indeed, that is their purpose.

This series of books examines the important and timely issue of the significance of arbitrary borders in history. Each volume focuses attention on a territorial division, but the analytical approach is more comprehensive. These studies describe arbitrary borders as places where people interact differently from the way they would if the boundary did not exist. This pattern is especially pronounced where there is no geographic reason for the boundary and no history recognizing its legitimacy. Even though many borders have been defined without legal precision, governments frequently have provided vigorous monitoring and military defense for them.

This series will show how the migration of people and exchange of goods almost always work to undermine the separation that borders seek to maintain. The continuing evolution of a European community provides a contemporary example illustrating this point, most obviously with the adoption of a single currency. Moreover, even former Soviet bloc nations have eliminated barriers to economic and political integration.

Globalization has emerged as one of the most powerful forces in international affairs during the twenty-first century. Not only have markets for the exchange of goods and services become genuinely worldwide, but instant communication and sharing of information have shattered old barriers separating people. Some scholars even argue that globalization has made the entire concept of a territorial nation-state irrelevant. Although the assertion is certainly premature and probably wrong, it highlights the importance of recognizing how borders often have reflected and affirmed the cultural, ethnic, or linguistic perimeters that define a people or a country.

Since the Cold War ended, competition over resources or a variety of interests threaten boundaries more than ever, resulting in contentious interaction, conflict, adaptation, and intermixture. How people define their borders is also a factor in determining how events develop in the surrounding region. This series will provide detailed descriptions of selected arbitrary borders in history with the objective of providing insights on how artificial boundaries separating people will influence international affairs during the next century.

Senator George J. Mitchell
September 2005

Introduction

James I. Matray
California State University, Chico

Throughout history, borders have separated people. Scholars have devoted considerable attention to assessing the significance and impact of territorial boundaries on the course of human history, explaining how they often have been sources of controversy and conflict. In the modern age, the rise of nation-states in Europe created the need for governments to negotiate treaties to confirm boundary lines that periodically changed as a consequence of wars and revolutions. European expansion in the nineteenth century imposed new borders on Africa and Asia. Many native peoples viewed these boundaries as arbitrary and, after independence, continued to contest their legitimacy. At the end of both world wars in the twentieth century, world leaders drew artificial and impermanent lines separating assorted people around the globe. Borders certainly are among the most important factors that have influenced the development of world affairs.

Chelsea House Publishers decided to publish a collection of books looking at arbitrary borders in history in response to the revival of the nuclear crisis in North Korea in October 2002. Recent tensions on the Korean peninsula are a direct consequence of Korea's partition at the 38th parallel at the end of World War II. Other nations in human history have suffered because of similar artificial divisions that have been the result of either international or domestic factors and often a combination of both. In the case of Korea, the United States and the Soviet Union decided in August 1945 to divide the country into two zones of military occupation ostensibly to facilitate the surrender of Japanese forces. However, a political contest was then underway inside Korea to determine the future of the nation after forty years of Japanese colonial rule. The Cold War then created two Koreas with sharply contrasting political, social, and economic systems that symbolized an ideological split among the Korean people. Borders separate people, but rarely prevent their economic, political, social, and cultural interaction. But in Korea, an artificial border has existed since 1945 as a nearly impenetrable barrier precluding meaningful contact between two portions of the same population. Ultimately, two authentic Koreas emerged, exposing how an arbitrary boundary can create circumstances resulting even in the permanent division of a homogeneous people in a historically united land.

Korea's experience in dealing with artificial division may well be unique, but it is not without historical parallels. The first group of books in this series on arbitrary boundaries provided description and analysis of the division of the Middle East after World War I, the Iron Curtain in Central Europe during the Cold War, the United States-Mexico Border, the 17th parallel in Vietnam, and the Mason-Dixon Line. Three authors in a second set of studies addressed the Great Wall in China, the Green Line in Israel, and the 38th parallel and demilitarized zone in Korea. Four other volumes described how discord over artificial borders in the Louisiana Territory, Northern Ireland, Czechoslovakia, and South Africa provide insights about fundamental disputes focusing on sovereignty, religion, and ethnicity. Six books now complete the series. Three authors explore the role of arbitrary boundaries in shaping the history of the city of London, the partition of British India, and the Tri-Border Region in Latin America. Finally, there are studies examining Britain's dispute with Spain over Gibraltar, Modern China, and the splintering of Yugoslavia after the end of the Cold War.

Admittedly, there are many significant differences between these boundaries, but these books will strive to cover as many common themes as possible. In so doing, each will help readers conceptualize how complex factors such as colonialism, culture, and economics determine the nature of contact between people along these borders. Although globalization has emerged as a powerful force working against the creation and maintenance of lines separating people, boundaries likely will endure as factors having a persistent influence on world events. This series of books will provide insights about the impact of arbitrary borders on human history and how such borders continue to shape the modern world.

James I. Matray
Chico, California
September 2005

1

Bombs
and
Borders

In 1990, after decades of turmoil, Argentina appeared to be on the verge of a new era. President Carlos Saúl Menem and his government pushed through a series of economic and political reforms that appeared to bring stability and prosperity to the country. A key component of this new era was the aggressive pursuit of foreign trade and investment. Currency reforms, reduced tariffs, and a scaled-back public sector made Argentina attractive to foreign companies, which helped the country expand and modernize its business sector.

This openness brought with it tragedy. On March 17, 1992, a suicide bomber drove a truck into the Israeli Embassy in Argentina's capital of Buenos Aires. The blast killed 29 people and injured 242 others. Two years later, on July 18, 1994, a second bomber detonated a van filled with explosives outside the offices of the Argentine-Israeli Mutual Aid Association, a cultural and community center in the capital. This attack killed three times as many people and injured hundreds more. Although the perpetrators behind both attacks were never arrested, a group calling itself "Islamic Jihad" claimed responsibility for the first attack.

According to Argentine security officials, Hezbollah, an Islamic organization based in Lebanon, was behind both attacks. In 1982, during the Lebanese Civil War, activists founded Hezbollah in reaction to Israel's invasion and occupation of southern Lebanon. Although its leaders defined it as a political and community organization, it recruited and trained soldiers for battle in the Middle East. It has also trained and funded terrorists who have gone on to attack targets throughout the world. Reportedly under the direction of Hezbollah officers, the bombings in Buenos Aires came in retaliation for Israeli actions against Lebanese and Palestinian activists.[1]

Security officials worked to identify the reasons that Argentina was the target of Islamic terrorists. Their investigations revealed that Jewish sites in their country were ideal targets. The end of military rule in 1984 had led to a contraction of the police and military forces that had once patrolled the country's borders. Lax enforcement of immigration laws made it relatively easy for foreign agents to enter and leave the country. Inconsistent inspections of imports helped terrorists transport the materials they used to build their bombs to Buenos Aires. In sum, for those who planned and committed these acts of terrorism, Argentina's borders were essentially transparent.[2]

The Argentine government worked hard to trace the route through which the terrorists traveled to their chosen targets. Initially, it blamed agents working for the Iranian Embassy for

A BRIEF HISTORY OF THE "PARTY OF GOD"

Hezbollah (also "Hizb Allah," and other variations), the "Party of God," first appeared in Lebanon in 1982. It developed within the Shi'a Muslim communities in response to the Israeli invasion. Organized as a local militia, with close ties to Iran and Syria, Hezbollah first operated exclusively as a military organization. It was dedicated to defending the ideals of revolution and resistance based on Islamic principles and inspired by the successful consolidation of an Islamic state in Iran after 1979. Its existence was revealed publicly in 1985, when its leaders announced their participation in the Lebanese National Resistance.

Hezbollah denies any connection with terrorism and advertises its commitment to the transformation of Lebanon into an Islamic state through peaceful, democratic efforts. It has funded the construction and operation of schools, medical clinics, and other social services, which has solidified public support for the organization and its political ambitions within the Shi'a community in Lebanon and among Lebanese exiles living abroad. Until 2000, however, when Israel withdrew its forces from southern Lebanon, its militia conducted a range of military operations against Israeli targets. Foreign observers have also tied the group to attacks against embassies and UN peacekeeping forces stationed in Lebanon and the region. The U.S. government has accused Hezbollah of executing two attacks against its embassy and of a 1983 suicide bomb attack against the U.S. Marine barracks in Beirut.

Hezbollah became an important minority party after it captured 12 seats in the Lebanese Parliament in the 1992 national elections. Its strong support of Syria has led many to question its political future in the wake of the 2005 Cedar Revolution, which helped end the Syrian occupation of Lebanon.

The tri-border region, pictured here in the lower right-hand corner of this map of Paraguay, is located on a bend in the Upper, or Alto, Paraná River in South America. Ciudad del Este, the second-largest city in Paraguay, is the area's economic center.

the attack. Journalists and other investigators implicated corrupt police officials. Later, the government would indict Lebanese nationals as the plot's masterminds, but other investigations connected the Syrian government with the attacks. As these allegations swirled, investigations identified an isolated corner of the country as the path through which the attackers traveled to their targets: the Triple Frontier or tri-border region, an area where trade and transit of goods and people flow with little regard for authority or national interest.

The tri-border region is located on a bend in the Upper, or Alto, Paraná River in South America. A place where the borders of Argentina, Brazil, and Paraguay meet, the area had been commonly known as the location of the world's greatest collection of waterfalls. Sparsely populated until recently, the local population is concentrated in three cities located within a few miles of each other across the river. More than 30,000 people live in the Argentine city of Puerto Iguazú, in the southern part of the region. Ciudad del Este, the second-largest city in Paraguay, is the area's economic center. Originally called "Puerto Stroessner," when government authorities first developed the site as a business area in 1957, the city quickly became known for its black market. Judging either by taxes collected or the value of business transacted, the businesses and economic activities centered in Ciudad del Este produce more revenue than the rest of Paraguay combined. An estimated 235,700 people live within the city.

Although the shops and stores of Ciudad del Este serve as the main source of employment, many workers live across the border in Foz do Iguaçú, Brazil. The Ponte da Amizade, or Friendship Bridge, connects the two cities, which lie less than a kilometer apart, across the Upper Paraná. With infrequent identity checks and with only a small force of border-patrol guards assigned to the job of inspecting the flow of tens of thousands of people across the bridge each day, the difficulties of living in one country and working in another are inconsequential. An estimated 300,000 people live in Foz do Iguaçú. Thousands more live in rural and suburban areas along the Brazilian side of the Alto Paraná River.

The three cities are linked by the roles they play in tourism and foreign trade. International airports and luxury hotels cater to foreign visitors from around the globe. Entrepreneurs in Paraguay and Brazil work to expand the exchange of goods and services that cross their common border. In recent years, a joint plan to exploit the hydroelectric potential of the Alto Paraná River has brought a significant increase in public-sector investment.

The creation of a South American Common Market, or Mercosur, in 1995, offered hopes for a brighter future.

The region's expanding economy and its potential for future growth have not reduced concerns about the area's problems, however. For many, the tri-border region now represents the gravest terrorist threat in the Western Hemisphere.

Speaking in October 2001 before a U.S. congressional committee charged with investigating the growth and spread of international terrorism, Ambassador Francis X. Taylor, who supervised the U.S. government's counterterrorism programs in South America, asserted that the tri-border region was a major base for Islamic terrorist organizations.[3] According to Taylor, the area harbored groups connected to the Shi'a branch of Islam (also known as "Shiite"), including Hezbollah, and provided funding for political and military organizations engaged in the struggle over Lebanon and Palestine. He also stated that Al-Gama'a al-Islamiyya, an organization that developed in Egypt and had been linked to attacks against tourists and government officials there, had ties to community organizations in Paraguay and Brazil, as well. Further, Taylor testified that Hamas, then an established threat to Israel's security, received significant support from residents of the tri-border region.

As investigations continued, possible connections between the terrorist attacks of September 11, 2001, and the tri-border region mounted. After interviewing local residents, Brazilian journalists reported that numerous al Qaeda operatives, including Khalid Sheikh Mohammed and Osama bin Laden, visited the area as recently as 1995. Terrorism experts and journalists continue to monitor the area. Each report underscores factors that make it attractive to planners and agents involved in this complex, multinational conflict.[4]

By the 1980s, the region attracted its first large group of refugees from the Middle East. Religious strife and political conflict had divided Lebanon in the early 1970s, which led to a civil war in 1975 and to an international conflict when Israeli leaders wanted to stabilize their northern borders. When the Israeli army invaded Lebanon in 1982, the destruction caused by warfare and the hope for a better life led many Lebanese to flee their homeland. The emigrants searched for areas that readily accepted foreigners and the Paraguayan and Brazilian frontier districts in the tri-border region became favored choices. The lax travel restrictions and visa requirements allowed the displaced to build homes and set up businesses quickly, first in Paraguay and later across the border in Brazil. Within a decade, immigrants from Lebanon and other parts of the Middle East had established large communities in the Argentine, Brazilian, and Paraguayan parts of the tri-border region.[5]

The new immigrants found wealth as agents in an international trading system. The tri-border region had developed into a major center for money laundering: Cash that Colombian drug lords made through the production and sale of cocaine flowed through the tourist agency offices and bank branches that sprung up throughout the region. Investigators asserted that the Lebanese immigrants soon expanded into other activities. The production and sale of counterfeit goods, such as designer clothing or bootleg compact discs, helped many of the new immigrants grow wealthy. Governments and local officials benefited from the spread of illegal activities. The simple act of smuggling cigarettes from one country, where taxes were low, to another, where taxes were higher, and underselling the local merchants, provided huge profits for the individuals who organized the trafficking of merchandise and the officials who accepted bribes in agreement to look the other way.[6]

The profits that legal and illegal trade created enriched the towns and cities of the tri-border region. The construction of mosques, which became the center of the Muslim communities there, symbolized the economic success that the immigrants had achieved. By 1990, the region had become a notorious center of counterfeiting and contraband trade. Local shops produced excellent copies of passports, driver's licenses, and other official documents for use by anyone who could afford to purchase them. By 1999, Argentine intelligence officials became convinced

Over the last two decades, the tri-border region has become a hotbed for international terrorist activities. The tri-border region has some 30,000 Muslim residents and is home to such Islamic terrorist groups as Hezbollah. Pictured here are two Paraguayan special police officers arresting an Arab resident of Ciudad del Este, shortly after the September 11, 2001, terrorist attacks on the United States.

that the tri-border region's connection to international terrorist groups was much deeper and more complex than previously thought. They uncovered and apparently halted a broad plan to attack sites in Canada and South America with ties to Israel or the United States.

With proof of a broader terrorist threat, the information investigators uncovered suggested an ominous shift: New organizations, with different ambitions and a longer list of enemies, joined Hezbollah in the tri-border region. Wire taps and surveillance reports asserted that al Qaeda agents had moved into the area. Like other groups, al Qaeda relied on the area's Islamic community for donations. Argentine officials accused the group of also using the area as a base for recruitment. Journalists in

Brazil and Paraguay asserted that military training camps operated in the jungle and forestlands along the unsettled Alto Paraná River. Donations from the Muslim communities of the tri-border region and the ease with which arms, ammunition, and other training materials could be smuggled into the area made these operations possible.

Additional evidence suggested that the established groups and al Qaeda organizers had set aside religious and ideological differences and launched new plots in cooperation with one another. This coordination of planning and resources made the tri-border region an extremely dangerous base. U.S. officials reported that the lack of strict immigration laws and ineffective enforcement of existing restrictions made the region a jumping-off point for terrorists with targets throughout the hemisphere. Once established in Paraguay or Brazil, terrorists could obtain false identification documents and then travel to other countries, where they launched attacks or joined clandestine "sleeper cells" and awaited instructions for future actions.

Plots against authorities across the hemisphere developed, and security forces found evidence that linked each to planners and bases in the tri-border region.[7] On November 28, 2000, Paraguayan authorities arrested Salah Abdul Karim Yassine in Ciudad del Este. Yassine was identified as an expert bomb-maker and was connected to al-Gama'a al-Islamiyya. He was first accused of plotting attacks against the American and the Israeli embassies in Asunción, Paraguay, but instead was charged with passport violations and deported to Egypt. On October 10, 2001, Mexican authorities arrested 10 suspected terrorists who they accused of planning an assassination attempt against Mexican president Vicente Fox. The group traveled to Mexico from the tri-border region and used false passports that they had obtained there.

Under pressure from the U.S. government, Paraguayan officials admitted publicly that their country had become the front line in the international war on terror. In a series of statements, officials asserted that terror groups moved organizers into the region in recent years. Working as religious teachers in association with the mosques in the tri-border region, suspected terrorists radicalized local youths, recruited new agents, and established cells for future operations. The Paraguayan government admitted that training bases existed in the sparsely populated rural areas along the Paraná and Paraguay rivers. Recruits received weapons training and indoctrination at these bases.

Journalists reported secret meetings that involved Taliban operatives and officers of al Qaeda. According to articles that appeared in 2002, a terrorist summit took place in a training camp on the border between Paraguay and Brazil.[8]

Further, the ready availability of false-identification documents allowed terrorists to blend in with the local community of peaceful, law-abiding Muslims. Housed safely and employed by small businesses that developed in the region, terrorists could easily move in and out of the tri-border region, return after completing missions, and await new orders.

Money laundering, long a major activity in the region, represents an additional concern for antiterrorist officials. Argentine, Brazilian, and Paraguayan authorities made a series of arrests in 2001 and 2002 that revealed the role Muslim immigrants played in such crimes. Officials accused the detainees of raising money for Hezbollah and al Qaeda. The cash they transferred came from a variety of activities: transporting drugs between Paraguay and Brazil, selling illegal copies of compact music disks (CDs) or movies on digital video disks (DVDs), and even through false sales of real estate in Lebanon to unsuspecting investors.

Local bank branches and foreign-exchange shops, which faced almost no restrictions on accepting deposits, exchanging currency, or transferring money abroad, facilitated the flow of cash from Latin America to the Middle East. This trade in cash has made Ciudad del Este one of the world's leading financial centers. While estimates vary, public officials calculated that the city's cash transactions average more than $10 billion each year. Most agree that the actual figure may be much larger. Legal and illegal commerce has produced a steady flow of remittances—as much as $500 million annually—to Islamic organizations based in the Middle East.[9]

In the United States, officials have urged the government to strengthen its ties with South American security forces and collectively fight terror in the region. To counter the relatively free flow of people, goods, and cash across the tri-border region, the U.S. government has proposed increased military aid and joint exercises with the region's police and military forces. In December 2003, representatives of the United States, Argentina, Brazil, and Paraguay formed the 3 + 1 Group on Tri-border Area Security, which took command of a coordinated effort to monitor and react to any future terrorist threats that develop in the region. The fluid borders of the Triple Frontier have made it one of the front lines of U.S. concern in reaction to Islamic terrorism since September 11, 2001.

Although many are happy with the increased security, this effort to transform the area's borders into effective barriers runs contrary to the region's history. For centuries, geography, demographics, material needs, and culture defined the borders of the region. These realities forged links that bind the peoples and places that make up the region—links that existed before the arrival of the first Europeans more than four centuries ago.

2

Beginnings

Although the fluid borders of the tri-border region are a product of history and politics, the area's geography laid the foundation for its creation. The region's geographic conditions both separate and connect it with the wider world. Geography also set the context for distinct patterns of settlement—centuries before the arrival of Europeans and their construction of the region's first political boundaries. The limits and the possibilities that the land presented shaped the communities that developed there in profound ways. In turn, the region's communities had little use for formal boundaries or borders. When European explorers moved to claim the region in their monarchs' names, the resulting political authority had little impact on the lives of the area's residents.

At the heart of the tri-border region is a set of rivers. The most important is the upper branch of the Paraná River, or the Alto Paraná. The Alto Paraná stretches from southeastern Brazil through the Pantanal wetlands south and then west. After joining with the Paraguay River, it continues south to the Río de la Plata and the Atlantic Ocean. Running roughly parallel, south of the Alto Paraná, is the Uruguay River. To the north, also on a roughly parallel course, is the Tebicuary River.

Two "departments" (states) within Paraguay that run north and west of the Alto Paraná River lie within the tri-border region: Alto Paraná and Itapúa. The terrain in this area is a mix of forest that thins to grassland as it runs west toward the Paraguay River. To the east, across the Alto Paraná River, in the western edge of the Brazilian states of Paraná and Mato Grosso, is Guairá, a thickly forested area. South of the river, in Argentina, lies Misiones, named for the Jesuit *reducciones*, or missions, that the religious order built to Christianize and "civilize" the native people of the tri-border region.

Unlike the Amazon or the Paraguay rivers, the Alto Paraná, the Uruguay, and the Tebicuary rivers are difficult to navigate. They are the best lines of transportation through the area, but during the wet season, from November to January, their rapids swell and their banks flood, wiping out many navigation markers that

Three tourists look out over the confluence of the Paraná and Iguassú rivers in Brazil. The rivers form a natural boundary, where Brazil, Argentina, and Paraguay come together to form the tri-border region.

make river transit safe. During the less frequent dry periods, the river levels drop and the rivers become impassible at a number of points.[10]

The climate in this area is tropical—between 67 and 71 inches (1,700 and 1,800 millimeters) of rain falls throughout the year. The temperature fluctuates little during most of the year. It is seldom too hot, and it cools in the evening. In winter, cold winds from the south are common but brief. The quality of the soil and the ample rain support a rich array of plant life. To the north and east of the tri-border region, thick forests make travel difficult. The land is higher in altitude—an extension of the Brazilian Highlands that stretches southwest from the Atlantic coast. Forests thin as one moves west into and through the tri-border area. Far to the west, past the Paraguay River, in the Gran Chaco, the land becomes barren and dry.[11]

Long before the arrival of the first Europeans, the region was a land of rich potential. Its first settlers might have perceived it as an island between desert, swamps, and thick forests. With plentiful game and ample opportunities to fish, the region might have seemed like an island perfect for settlement.

Geography isolated the tri-border region from areas of earlier settlement, however. The Chaco provided a forbidding barrier that separated the urban centers of the Incas and their predecessors from the Alto Paraná basin. The lush and wet Pantanal, far to the north, discouraged passage from the northern reaches of the continent. The rivers facilitated travel into the region, but the eastern forests discouraged exploration and delayed settlement.

Archaeological evidence suggests that the tri-border region's first settlers moved west from lands near the coast of Brazil. They arrived centuries before the Europeans, moving along the banks of the area's rivers and through the forests of the Brazilian Highlands, but the exact date of their first settlement is unknown. The region's pre-Columbian residents are all broadly identified as Guaraní. Four main Amerindian groups took up residence in distinct areas. The Cario settled north and west of the Tebicuary River and east of the Paraguay River. The Itatine lived in the southeastern corner of Paraguay north and west of the Alto Paraná River. The Guairá lived west of the Alto Paraná in the more densely forested lands of the region. The Tapé lived south of the Alto Paraná.[12]

A few allies and many enemies surrounded the settled Guaraní peoples. The Payaguas were sometimes allies and sometimes enemies of the Carios. During drier months, they created compounds near the edge of the Paraguay River. When the rivers rose, the Payaguas would gather their possessions and live on the river, fishing and trading with friendly settlements to support themselves. Farther north, near the Alto Paraná River, the forest was too dense for settlement. The Aches, also defined as part of the Guaraní culture, lived in this area as nomads, hunting and gathering to support their communities.

Chaco tribes, called Guaycurú by the Guaranís and, later, the

Spanish, conducted frequent raids from the Chaco across the Paraguay River and sometimes far into the tri-border region. To the north, the equally hostile Mbayos made the Brazilian forests a dangerous place for hunters.

Although each group had territories it defined and defended, designated borders did not yet exist. The rivers provided some separation, but food, fuel, and other necessities encouraged raids, forced migrations, and sparked wars. Weather and the migration of fish and game determined where and when settlements were built or disbanded. With thick forests and harsh deserts separating the region from areas with more settled populations, the area remained isolated from any American empire that might have defined boundaries or set borders.

Ringed by enemies, the Guaranís designed their settlements for defense. A trench, wall, or fence protected the compound and provided protection for defenders. The Guaranís lived in large huts that sheltered multiple generations of extended families. A village had four or more of these large huts, with a number of families all living communally in a single dwelling. The residents of a given hut shared a founding ancestor, and their relationships and status were determined by family lines passed from father to son.[13] Each hut had a chief, who organized the space the families shared. Families related to the chief produced food for him. He, in turn, led during times of war and, some evidence suggests, served as a shaman or religious figure for his followers. Chiefs had a number of wives, as did other men within the community.[14]

The Guaranís were not nomadic—they engaged in farming as well as hunting and trading for material support, but their settlements were not permanent. The settlers cleared their farmland by slashing and burning the existing bushes and trees. They worked the land with simple tools. They farmed manioc, corn, and other staples for a few years until the fertility of the land declined. When the promise of good harvests faded, the settlers abandoned their chosen site and moved on to start anew.[15]

In this manner, the Guaranís had only a loose connection

Three Guaraní men build the framework for a house in Brazil. Traditionally, multiple generations of extended families lived in each house, and a chief, who organized the space the families shared, in turn, protected them.

with a specific territory. Their relation to their extended family, with whom they shared their living quarters, or their loyalty to the tribe defined their identity. Borders and boundaries between Guaraní territory and that of their rivals was not firmly established. Instead, political identity and allegiance rose out of a sense of community and a connection to shared ancestors. The chiefs and councils focused on controlling and protecting resources, not on defining and defending set territories.

The transitory nature of even the settled Guaraní communities contributed to the generalization of warfare in the tri-border region. Invaders attacked Guaraní settlements for captives, food, and other resources. In response, the Guaranís launched raids against their enemies. The violence of intertribal relations helped make the tri-border region stand out from adjacent areas. Most tribes that lived along the river basins or in deserts

or forests reacted violently to visitors. The Carios and other settled groups operated from a position of relative strength. They
could afford to assess strangers and their intentions. They
attacked those they judged dangerous and negotiated with those
who offered something that might benefit the community.

Through the eyes of the Europeans who first arrived in the tri-
border region in the sixteenth century, the Guaraní settlements

A COMMUNITY THAT SHIFTS WITH THE CURRENT

In comparison to the deserts, jungles, and thick forests that surrounded the
area, Europeans regarded the tri-border region as "settled." By European
standards, however, the indigenous settlers were only loosely tied to the land.
In response to the weather and the presence of game, Guaraní settlements
moved frequently. Hence, the concepts of borders and boundaries that mattered so much to the European invaders were entirely alien to them. One
European observer provided this account of a particularly mobile community
that lived in the region:

When the waters are low, the people from the interior come and live on the
banks of the river with their wives and children, and pass their time in fishing,
for the fish are abundant and very fat at this season. They live pleasant lives,
dancing and singing the day and night, like persons who are relieved from all
anxiety about food; but when the waters begin to rise, which is in January, they
retire inland, because at that season the floods begin, and the waters rise six
fathoms above the banks of the river. . . . At such times the natives keep very
large canoes in readiness for this emergency; and in the middle of these canoes
they throw two or three loads of mud, and make a hearth. The Indian then enters
with his wife, children, and household goods, and floats on the rising tide wher-
ever they like. He lights a fire on the hearth to cook his food and for warmth, and
thus he voyages for four months of the year, or as long as the floods last. . . .*

* Luis L. Domínguez, "Conquest of the River Plate 1525–1555." In John H. Parry and Robert Keith, eds.,
trans. *New Iberian World: A Documentary History of the Discovery and Settlement of Latin America to the
Early 17th Century*. Vol. 5. New York: Times Books, 1984, pp. 290–291.

would seem like tranquil islands in comparison to the less friendly lands farther south. The Guaranís had established important precedents that would influence the development of the region in the coming centuries. They had created a material foundation for the region's economy. By clearing the land and building settlements, they established a more dynamic economy based on farming and trade. As their population expanded, the Guaranís were better able to defend their settlements from outsiders. For Spanish invaders, the presence of settled towns had another purpose. This population would serve as the initial foundation for the development of commercial activities that would tie the region to the developing Spanish empire in the Americas.

Nevertheless, the process of developing the lands of the tri-border region created circumstances that resisted integration and definition. Although they shared a language and certain cultural practices, political authority under the Guaranís was splintered, dispersed, and localized. Farming practices required the movement of settlement sites at regular intervals. Consequently, any sense of boundaries or borders remained flexible and fluid. It would be the Europeans who would make the first significant attempt to draw boundary lines in the region.

3

European
Settlement

Europeans "discovered" the American continents between 1492 and 1500. Christopher Columbus, sponsored by the rulers of the Spanish Kingdoms of Castille and Aragón, sought new avenues for trade. Vasco da Gama and his Portuguese expedition made landfall for the first time in Brazil. Together, they launched the encounter between the Old and New worlds. After explorations mapped the territory and revealed the resources of the newly discovered lands, the potential existed for conflict between Spain and Portugal.

A compromise reached in 1494 with the intervention of the papacy, however, produced the Treaty of Tordesillas. With only vague knowledge of the territories involved and well before the concept of the American continents' very existence emerged, the rivals set a line between Spanish and Portuguese possessions. The treaty divided the Atlantic Ocean and the lands of the "new world" between the two imperial Catholic kingdoms, along a line set 370 leagues, or 1,100 miles, west of the Cape Verde Islands (off the West African coast), which Portugal had colonized. This line was the first formal—and completely arbitrary—boundary imposed on the Americas by Europeans. It served its purpose, and Spain and Portugal avoided war, but ambitions and realities quickly made the treaty outdated. In this new world, Portugal was relegated to the area now known as Brazil.

In fact, the two kingdoms avoided conflict by fortune and default. Portugal took charge of the ocean routes between western and southern Africa. Building trading posts and launching convoys, the Portuguese developed markets that fully commanded the resources and attention of the Crown. When Portuguese expeditions took charge of the Arabian Sea and the Indian Ocean, Portugal became Europe's best source of Asian products. The development of its Asian and African trading links would consume what resources the Portuguese Crown had at its disposal for exploration and conquest. As a result of a disappointing initial exploration of Brazil's coast, and in deference to the requirements of the Treaty of Tordesillas, Portugal essentially left the Americas to the Spanish.

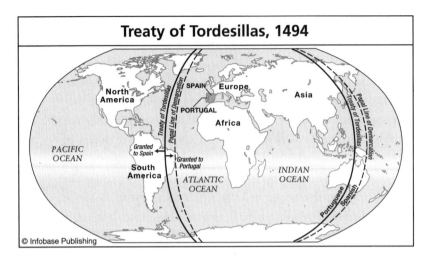

In 1494, the Treaty of Tordesillas mandated that the world outside of Europe would be divided between Spain and Portugal along a north-south meridian 1,100 miles west of the Cape Verde Islands. The line of demarcation was orginally created by Pope Alexander VI in 1493, in return for Spain's and Portugal's promise to Christianize all newly discovered lands. This map shows the two lines of demarcation and both countries' sphere of influence.

After signing the treaty in 1494, Spanish officials largely ignored the boundary that separated Spanish and Portuguese zones. As explorers stumbled across the islands and continents of the Americas, they surveyed and claimed territories as they saw fit. The Spanish, like the Portuguese, hoped to find an ocean route to Asia that would open up their own trading system. Within two decades of Columbus's initial expedition, the Spanish Crown and *conquistadores* focused on the potential wealth that American lands might produce.[16]

New expeditions came to the Caribbean and the South Atlantic in the years that followed. Juan Díaz de Solís traveled to the Río de la Plata in 1516. With the hope that the estuary was a route through the continent, the expedition made landfall. Solís and his soldiers encountered an overwhelming number of Charrúa warriors, who slaughtered the invaders. The loss forced the survivors to abandon further explorations. By accident, the Solís expedition led to the first European visit to the Alto Paraná

River basin. On its return to Spain, one of the expedition's ships ran aground on an island. Lacking sufficient space or supplies to transport all of the shipwrecked adventurers, a number remained on the island, which they named Santa Catalina. The local tribes proved friendly and supportive. Vague attempts at communication revealed a fantastic story to the visitors. The locals stated that a wealthy and powerful kingdom existed far to the west. Ruled by a fair-skinned king, this realm was rich in gold, silver, and other goods beyond the Europeans' imaginations.

The story captivated at least one of the shipwrecked invaders. Alejo García, a Portuguese sailor who traveled with the Solís expedition on contract, decided to search for this kingdom. He convinced a small group of Europeans to accompany him, and, according to his reports, his party and about 2,000 tribespeople set off on an expedition to the interior. In 1524, García began the march from the coast of what is today the southernmost state in Brazil; Rio Grande do Sul, and continued across Paraná to Mato Grosso. Struggling through dense forests and across marshes and rivers, the expedition moved across the Alto Paraná River. Their ambition to find the rumored kingdom made the area's small settlements uninteresting to García and his men. Pushing westward, the expedition eventually encountered trouble. Before crossing the Paraguay River, hostile tribes scattered and then attacked the invaders. García and his supporters nevertheless recovered gold, silver, and textiles, which they perceived to be from the land they sought.

García and his party returned successfully to the coast, where they passed on news of their discoveries to Spanish officials. The expedition did not, however, lead to a Spanish invasion of the tri-border region. At roughly the same time that García made his way through the forests between Paraguay and Brazil, Francisco Pizarro and a separate Spanish expedition made contact with the Inca Empire. The establishment of Spanish control over the rich and complex Andean communities that the Incas had organized gave Spain a base for its operations in South

America. García might have pressed to lead another exploration to the region, but a dispute with Guaraní allies led to his death in 1525.

The Venetian explorer Sebastián Gaboto led a second expedition to the Río de la Plata region in 1526. Again, Spain had no desire to settle the area. Gaboto, better known as Sebastian Cabot, instead planned to map the region and to find a route through South America. The expedition stopped at Santa Catalina Island, where survivors of the García expedition convinced Cabot and his men to travel up the Paraná River to search for the kingdom that the Guaranís had described. At first, the local tribes received the European explorers peacefully, but tensions rose as time passed, and, in 1528, Guaraní warriors ambushed a Spanish party. No longer welcome and with river travel along all northern routes blocked by impassible rapids, waterfalls, and shallows, the expedition returned to Spain in 1529.

Portugal's preoccupation with Africa and Asia meant that Brazil remained largely unexplored. In turn, because the area seemed to offer little, the Spanish ignored their sections of the tri-border region. Spain's conquest of central Mexico and the Andes allowed it to focus its imperial efforts on areas where large, organized populations produced mineral and agricultural goods for the European market. The sparse population of the tri-border region, which was isolated from silver mines and rich, productive lands, did not entice Spanish officials. More than a decade passed before Spanish explorers returned.[17]

After 1500, the Portuguese Crown turned over authority for the exploration and development of Brazilian lands to *capitanes* (private citizens who had purchased or who had been granted authority over territories, called captaincies, in Brazil), but the assignments had produced little. Spanish officials, nonetheless, had concerns that Portugal might establish a claim on the Río de la Plata region. To head off this remote threat, the Spanish Crown commissioned Pedro de Mendoza to be the governor of a large, well-funded expedition in 1535. Mendoza crossed the

Atlantic with 1,500 settlers and soldiers. Delays and a brief rebellion threatened the operation, but by February 1536 the group entered the estuary. After searching for a proper site, Mendoza ordered the establishment of the town of Santa María del Buen Aire, on the southern banks of the Río de la Plata.

Initially, the colonists made some progress, but the size of the settlement created problems. The supplies the colonists brought with them ran out quickly. Trade with the locals provided no help. Unlike the Guaranís, who initially accepted García and his party in peace, the tribes that lived on the plains surrounding Buenos Aires attacked the settlement. Forays in search of game were dangerous and farming nearly impossible. The settlers quickly found it difficult to meet even their most basic needs for food and other supplies.

Governor Mendoza authorized explorations of the rivers leading north out of the estuary in the first months following the establishment of the settlement. One expedition, led by Juan de Ayolas and Domingo Martínez de Irala, survived successive attacks as it traveled north along the Paraná River. Ordered to locate a better base for explorations of the interior, its commanders selected a site on the eastern bank of the Paraná.

When it became clear that the settlers of Santa María del Buen Aire could not hold out any longer against their adversaries, Mendoza authorized a move to the new and more promising site. The second settlement became Asunción, the future capital of Paraguay. The Cario tribes that lived in the area surrounding the site were grateful hosts. Having engaged in generations of conflict with surrounding tribes that launched raids from the west and the south, the Carios were willing to make an alliance with the Spanish survivors. This alliance gave the Spanish a military force that dominated the region. Campaigns into the Chaco and along the Paraguay and Paraná River basins helped secure a transit route into the Atlantic. The alliance also served as the basis of a distinct community that spread south and west of Asunción.

A mixing of peoples and cultures occurred in most of Spanish

America. In Asunción, the Spanish survivors and the local elite merged. Spaniards assumed titles of authority within the Guaraní culture. In turn, the mixed-raced, or *mestizo*, children

COMMON ENEMIES

Domingo Martínez de Irala emerged as the leader of the Spanish settlers in Asunción. After the abandonment of Buenos Aires in 1537, Asunción became the only successful Spanish settlement in South America prior to the conquest of the Inca Empire.

The following selection from Irala's *Memoria* provides an early description of the native peoples and their difficult relations with the European invaders. This selection highlights the ways in which the Spaniards relied on the indigenous peoples of the region in a unique manner that shaped the development of Asunción and the tri-border region for centuries. This relationship forged a bond between European and American worlds unlike any other in Spanish or Portuguese America.

We hold the Guarani or Cario Indians who live for thirty leagues around [Asunción] as vassals of His Majesty, and both they and their wives serve the Christians in all the things they need; 700 women have gone to serve the Christians in their fields and their houses, and because of their work and especially because it was God's pleasure, there is such an abundance of food that there is enough not only for the people who live there but for another 3,000 in addition. Whenever it is necessary to make war, 1,000 Indians join our company in their canoes, and if we wish to take them overland, we take as many as we want with God's help. And with the help of these Indians, we have overcome many tribes of other Indians who have not been friendly. . . . We have gone farther inland by land toward the west or northwest, where we found so many people that it seems to me that we are too few to attack them. . . .

All the Indians who live along the banks of [the Paraná] farther up are not people who cultivate the soil or live in organized towns. Great care has to be taken with them, especially when trading. . . . One should guard against the Guaranies of the Islands and the Quirandies in everything, since they are our mortal enemies.*

---

* Domingo Martínez de Irala, "Memoria" (1541). In John H. Parry and Robert Keith, eds., trans., *New Iberian World: A Documentary History of the Discovery and Settlement of Latin America to the Early 17th Century*. Vol. 5. New York: Times Books, 1984, pp. 274–275.

of Spanish survivors and elite Guaraní women gained full admittance to the Spanish world. Their fathers recognized their legitimacy and passed on their titles and status. Although exposure to European diseases and exploitation by Spanish authorities cut down the indigenous population (which fell to less than 10 percent of its size within a century after the Spanish arrived), mestizos slowly took their place in the culture, and a blended society developed. This set the region apart from the rest of South America, where the American and European ways and practices remained much more distinct for generations.[18]

Local conditions and distant developments transformed Asunción and the tri-border region. The governors tried to promote Spanish culture, but the distance between Asunción and other colonial cities left the settlement isolated. Asunción's population grew slowly, and its authority over the people living in surrounding areas, who continued to live as they had before the Spaniards' arrival, remained weak. In turn, the threat of invasion by indigenous groups forced cooperation. Spanish officers led Guaraní armies against shared enemies. Isolation and cooperation helped define the region as culturally and socially distinct. As geography had separated the Guaranís from other American empires and cultures, geography set a boundary that made the tri-border region unique within the developing Spanish-American empire.

The blended cultural, social, and material world that slowly developed in the land between the Paraná and Paraguay rivers benefited the Spanish settlers. Pedro de Mendoza, after ordering the abandonment of Santa María del Buen Aire, decided to return to Spain. He was ill when he left South America, and he died en route. Martínez de Irala succeeded Mendoza as governor. Under his authority, Asunción organized the Guaraní communities into a capable workforce that produced more than enough food, clothing, and other supplies for the growing colony. Local products soon found markets in other parts of South America. "Paraguayan tea," in particular, grew popular with the laborers in the mining districts of Bolivia and Peru:

Dried and crushed, the leaves of the yerba mate tree made a caffeinated drink, called "mate," which was served like tea.

Perhaps more important, the combination of Spanish arms and tactics with the numbers of Guaraní men drafted from outlying settlements led to the creation of a significant military force that pacified the lower and upper Paraná River basins. Raids against enemy settlements allowed Asunción to sponsor a resettlement of the lower Río de la Plata estuary, which culminated in the reestablishment of Buenos Aires in 1580.

Although it never approached the wealth of Lima, the capital of the Spanish colonial enterprise in South America, Asunción developed a resource that would help it grow and prosper far beyond the other towns and outposts that developed between the Andes and the Atlantic: a settled and exploitable labor force.

Because of the colony's distant and isolated location, the Spanish Crown also issued the Royal *Cédula* of 1537. This decree gave the citizens of Asunción the privilege of electing a governor to run Paraguay until a replacement appointed by the Crown arrived to fill any vacancy. In the years that followed, the citizens of Asunción argued that they had the right to choose their governors, which encouraged a sense of autonomy among the settlers.

Following Crown procedures, Governor Martínez de Irala awarded *encomiendas* (grants of land and people) to the men of Asunción's most important Spanish families. These awards put one or more Guaraní settlements in the hands of the grantees. Those who controlled an encomienda controlled the labor of the settlements under their authority. (The practice was similar to the European feudal system of forced labor.) With available labor, the grantees took charge of the supply of food, clothing, and other staples. They also opened up new mercantile industries: ranching, tanning, the production of yerba mate, and the collection of wood for fuel, construction, and other uses.

The encomienda grants cemented the elite position of the Spanish invaders and their descendants in the generations that followed. This exploitation concerned Spanish authorities. In 1542, the Crown appointed Álvar Núñez Cabeza de Vaca as Asunción's new governor. Cabeza de Vaca came with orders to abolish the encomienda system and to bring under his own supervision the mercantile activities of the region. His efforts to assert royal authority went against the autonomy to which the local elite had become accustomed and also against their ambitions. Consequently, on April 25, 1544, about 200 members of the Asunción elite rebelled against the governor. They arrested Cabeza de Vaca and held him in prison until they arranged safe passage for him to Spain.

Spanish authorities crossed a border created by Asunción's isolation. The settlers' collective experience had created a separate world, with its own distinct political order. Citing the Royal Cédula of 1537, the rebels elected their own governor: Martínez de Irala. Disagreements that separated the town's elite families into rival political factions soon led to a period of instability. Temporarily freed from Spanish supervision, the citizens of Asunción tried to extend their control over Guaraní laborers. This change in the encomienda system provoked a strong reaction. A string of rebellions culminated in an uprising in 1560 that involved every settlement in the region and nearly destroyed the colony.[19]

The establishment and development of Asunción by Spain set in motion a number of conflicts that would, over the centuries, challenge the European nation's claim of authority over the Paraná River basin. Initially, because of Portugal's disinterest, what would become the tri-border region was under Spanish control. The successful exploitation of the area's resources, however, attracted explorers and invaders from Brazil. Searching for slaves and for marketable goods, after 1545, raiders from the coast attacked Guaraní settlements with greater frequency. As the raids grew, tensions between Spanish and Portuguese authorities mounted.

Consequently, before the first wave of European exploration and settlement of the tri-border region had come to a close, the question of who controlled this land and its people fell into dispute. In addition to the contest between the Iberian kingdoms, historical developments complicated the political and material map of the region in other ways, as well.

Asunción was the product of an expedition from Spain that targeted the Río de la Plata region for conquest, exploration, and settlement. As Buenos Aires failed, Asunción prospered. Legally, its subjects were ruled by authorities in Lima, the capital of the viceroyal government that ruled over Spanish South America. Communication with Lima, however, was difficult. Overland travel brought the possibility of encountering warriors from unconquered tribes. Travel by sea was long, dangerous, and infrequent. With communication through established channels not secure, the residents of Asunción came to rely on their own efforts, as well as their own interpretations of colonial policy.

The question of who ruled over whom did not become clearer with the passage of time. As Spain's colonial system developed, bureaucrats in Lima became more jealous of Spanish authority and more arbitrary in their own rulings. The development of other towns and cities complicated matters. Buenos Aires, rebuilt by an expedition sent from Asunción, replaced the Paraguayan town as the key base for Spanish defense against Brazil and other foreign groups that the Spanish Crown considered a threat. Asunción would continue to provide the military resources to answer all threats, but Buenos Aires had the advantage of being closer to Spain. The rise of Córdoba—at the midpoint of a wagon road that connected Buenos Aires to Spain's Andean colonies and towns—as the center of Church operations east of the Andes created a second rival to Asunción.

In reaction to the rise of other cities to prominence within the colonial system, the citizens of Asunción grew more autonomous. The area's first boundaries, established by its geography, helped define the lifeways of the first settlers. Spanish invaders fit into the cultural, social, and material lines that separated the area from the Atlantic and the Pacific. Within generations, isolation encouraged autonomy, and a practical political boundary joined the borders already set by the merging of Spanish and American worlds. The locals assumed authority over what would one day be the tri-border region.

4

Jesuits and the Guaranís

The borders that defined the Triple Frontier after the first generation of the colonial era came as a result of arbitrary imposition and local realities. Europeans, concerned with the privileges of colonial enterprise, imposed authority in an effort to monopolize the profits that the indigenous labor and international commerce might produce. These impositions existed in legal theory. In practice, they had little influence over what happened in Asunción and its surrounding territories. The official border between Spanish Paraguay and Portuguese Brazil remained, in fact, uncharted throughout the colonial era. Local forces, however, sought to control the territory. They organized labor, exploited the land, and developed industry to fulfill their own desires. Brazilians plunged through the forests that separated Paraguay from the Atlantic in pursuit of their own interests: slaves and plunder. The pursuit of wealth created conflict within the tri-border region. As the conflict developed, the cultural, social, and material distinctions took precedence over the official borders of the region.

In the territories of the Paraguay and Upper Paraná river basins, isolation and existing practices led to a blending of American and European traits. This blending created a unique society that set the area apart from the rest of Spanish and Portuguese America. With Spanish authorities focused on the complex and rich central Andes, and the Portuguese presence concentrated on Brazil's Atlantic coastline, the blended communities in and near what would become the tri-border region became accustomed to autonomy.

Spanish and Guaraní traditions did blend, but the establishment of a new mestizo, or mixed-race, elite produced resentment and resistance within the Guaraní settlements. Labor drafts, efforts by the descendants of Spanish invaders to take control of more and more land, and the concentration of political power in the hands of a few privileged families created tensions. Five times between 1539 and 1600, Guaraní communities rebelled against local authorities. Although the authorities successfully turned back each revolt, lingering tensions led Spanish

Crown officials to consider new policies. When rebellions failed to improve conditions for the Guaranís under Spanish control, many individuals and families simply moved away from Asunción and its environs. For these displaced people, the Alta Paraná River basin provided isolation and escape. The new settlements created there maintained wary relations with the Spanish, as they developed what would become the tri-border region to meet their needs.

Although the Portuguese had no desire to compete with the Spanish for settlements in the area, the Portuguese presence did pose a second set of problems for Spain and its loyal subjects in Paraguay. *Bandeirantes*—traveling bands of raiders and explorers—scouted the interior of the continent in search of valuable resources. They valued jewels, gold, and other precious commodities, but they mainly sought slaves. Raiding Amerindian villages and bounding prisoners for eventual sale to landowners and merchants in the coastal towns of Brazil had developed into the most secure and lucrative business for these bands of privateers.[20] The threat of bandeirante raids was a constant problem. The Guaraní settlements, populated by men, women, and children who had already become familiar with European ways of life and work, were extremely attractive. Equally important to Crown officials, however, was that the actual boundary between Portuguese and Spanish territories in South America remained uncharted.

The solution for these challenges came slowly. Taking the initiative, the Spanish Crown authorized the creation of Jesuit missions in the area. The Jesuit Order had received its commission as a part of the Catholic Church's efforts to combat the loss of faithful parishioners to the Protestant movement of the Reformation in 1540. Jesuits, well-trained and loyal to the Catholic Church, adopted a number of strategies to keep Catholics from leaving the Church. Jesuits served as advisors to rulers, they established colleges to train new clergy, and they worked in urban and frontier areas in every settled region to build up the number of practicing Catholics.[21]

During the early part of the seventeenth century, the Jesuits, a religious order of the Catholic Church, established a number of successful missions in the tri-border region. Jesuit priests at each mission set out to spread European culture and Christianity to the natives of the region. Pictured here is the Sao Miguel Mission, just south of the tri-border region, in Brazil.

During the early part of the seventeenth century, the Jesuits established a number of successful missions in the tri-border region. Missions were compounds built in areas that were new to the Catholic faith. These operations provided religious instruction and taught practical skills, such as tanning, the production of textiles, farming, or managing livestock, to Indians who resided or worked in the mission. The goods produced by the mission population were sold locally, and the profits the sales generated helped support Jesuit activities throughout the world.

The Jesuits first arrived in Paraguay in 1588. Like the Franciscan missionaries before them, the Jesuits initially worked in and around Asunción. Individual priests traveled north along the Paraguay River and east across the Alto Paraná River to Guairá. Others helped expand Church operations in the city of Asunción. They established a college and a church and served as confessors for many of the town's elite. While the Jesuits helped meet the religious and educational needs of Asunción's isolated residents, they also took the lead in introducing Catholic doctrine and European habits among the Guaraní settlements across the region.

The Spanish Crown agreed to let the Jesuit Order establish missions in the Paraguay and Alto Paraná river basins. Each mission would work toward converting Guaraní settlements into Europeanized towns. The mission staff would accelerate the spread of European culture and lifestyle among the Indians. As the missions grew and spread, the missionaries would help develop local industry and mercantile trade. Finally, the missions would create a clear line between Spanish and Portuguese territories and give Crown officials greater control over this undeveloped and isolated frontier.

This decision represented an official recognition of the failure of treaties and edicts to define and confirm Spanish authority over the tri-border region. The Jesuits, through the promotion of European cultural norms and practices—including religion, styles of dress, forms of work, and the fine arts—would break down the boundary that separated the isolated mestizo world, which controlled the land between the Paraguay and Paraná rivers, from that of the Spanish. As the locals became more Europeanized, the Spanish Crown's ambitions to take charge and define the area's cultural, social, and material borders would gain ground.

The Jesuits built their first missions in Guairá, west of the Alto Paraná River, in 1610. The missionaries' knowledge of local languages helped them establish good relations with the tribes in the area. Once accepted by the locals, the Jesuits selected sites for the mission compounds. Loreto, the first mission built in Guairá, closely followed the pattern of the cities that the Spanish had laid out throughout the Americas: square in shape, with an open plaza at the center, and the chapel set as the focus of the compound. Workshops, residences for the missionaries and the Amerindians, and storage sheds ringed the center.

The Jesuits chose sites near Guaraní settlements. This choice was in part practical: The missions had to be where the "innocents" lived. In addition, missions located far from Spanish settlements operated with fewer bureaucratic and political constraints. In effect, the Jesuits chose to operate within the boundaries of the American world and outside those that the Spanish hoped to impose. The Jesuits' selection of sites for the missions led to problems: Many were subject to flooding and other unhealthy conditions. Although climate and weather created challenges, the missionaries did make progress with their charges.

Ideally, each mission operated self-sufficiently. Using the labor of the mission subjects, or neophytes, missionaries developed farming, ranching, and other industries that supported the community's needs. The training helped teach the neophytes European ways of living and working. The mission operations revealed the Jesuit ambitions: They had promised to civilize the natives and to make the border between Spanish and Portuguese territories clear and secure. The missionaries, however, worked to isolate their charges. Mission fathers provided religious instruction and vocational training in Guaraní, not Spanish. Although the requirements of the faith forced the neophytes to change many of their customs and habits, the missionaries wanted to protect the Guaranís from the corrupting aspects of European society.

Despite the challenges nature presented, the missions quickly transformed the Guairá territory. Mission farms and workshops were productive enough to produce surpluses. In particular, the missions developed the yerba mate industry to new levels. Yerba mate trees grew wild in the woods north and east of Asunción. To make yerba mate, teams of foragers had to travel to the woods and gather the leaves. In a process that took weeks, the foragers dried the leaves, then crushed and bagged them for transport back to Asunción.

Spanish settlers and their descendants relied on the encomienda system to provide them with the laborers necessary for the harvesting of yerba mate. The small groups of encomienda-bound laborers could not match the larger and better organized teams of neophytes that the Jesuits led into the forests. Initially, the market for yerba mate was large enough for the settlers and the Jesuits to share. Yerba mate was popular in all the growing towns of South America. As the missions expanded their production, the competition began to anger the settlers. The demand for high-quality "Paraguayan Tea" increased in the mining districts of Bolivia and Peru. The Jesuits operated independently of the markets that the Crown and Lima-based merchant houses controlled. They declared that they produced goods for market only to support their missions, colleges, and clergy. The settlers disagreed: They believed the Jesuits wanted to monopolize control of the yerba mate trade.

The Jesuits had hoped to isolate the region from the Spanish world. Unfortunately, the success of their missions attracted greater attention from the Portuguese. Large bands of invaders attacked the 13 Guairá missions between 1619 and 1631. These missions had created a skilled workforce, and the bandeirantes captured Guaraní adults and children and marched them off to the slave markets of coastal Brazil. Although initial raids led to the capture of hundreds of neophytes, the danger grew. In 1628, an army of 3,000 attacked mission after mission. The raiders destroyed the compounds and killed all those who were too old to be sold profitably as slaves. In 1631, raiders attacked Spanish towns as well as missions.

To avoid a total disaster, the Jesuits decided to flee with the surviving mission population. Forcing the neophytes to travel with them, the missionaries moved south and west. Stopping between the Paraná and Uruguay rivers, the Jesuits selected sites for a new string of missions. Learning from past mistakes, the mission fathers selected sites close to water sources on high ground that were not only less prone to flooding but also were removed from swampland. The new missions had a design similar to the old ones. Each was built as a fort, though, to protect against Portuguese slave raiders.

The Jesuits established new farming and pastureland. They also developed new yerba mate plantations that quickly made the new missions productive and profitable. By recruiting new converts from local settlements and moving subject populations from lands north of Asunción to the new sites, the missionaries expanded the depleted neophyte ranks. By 1710, the Jesuits ran 30 missions and supervised more than 100,000 Guaranís.[22]

The Jesuits also expanded the neophytes' training to include military drills and combat tactics. To protect their religious operations, they petitioned Crown officials in Spain to permit the training of neophytes as soldiers. They also asked permission to buy weapons, gunpowder, and other essential supplies. The settlers in Asunción viewed the training and arming of neophytes as a risky endeavor, but Crown officials believed that, with the Portuguese threat mounting, there was no alternative. In 1645, the viceregal government sent arms and munitions to the missions. Even before they received permission from the Spanish Crown, the Jesuits began the training of a large and skilled militia. Initially, the Guaraní troops faced down Amerindian attacks and occasional Portuguese raids. Soon, however, the Jesuits chose to attack the bases of the Portuguese raiders. Jesuit missionaries led Guaraní cavalry and foot soldiers into Portuguese territory on numerous campaigns.[23]

The creation of such a powerful military force fundamentally transformed the region. The actions of the Jesuits effectively blocked the Portuguese invasions into the land that Spanish authorities claimed, but the Jesuits did not help establish colonial borders that served Spanish interests. Instead, the missions promoted lines of separation between the mercantile world based in Asunción and the missions themselves. Granted the right to pacify and civilize the area, the Jesuits introduced an entirely new project—to set a border between Spanish America and its "millennial kingdom."

The Jesuits in the tri-border region pursued an ambitious policy that helped separate their mission operations from both Spanish authority and Portuguese incursions. They secured judgments from courts and councils in Spain that extended and preserved their control over the Guaraní settlements along the Paraná River. They developed their mercantile industries independent of

BISHOP BERNARDINO DE CÁRDENAS AND THE "KINGDOM OF THE JESUITS"

Many individuals resented the power and wealth of the Jesuits, but perhaps none more than Bernardino de Cárdenas. He was trained by the Franciscan Order and gained experience as an administrator and parish organizer in Lima during the early seventeenth century. In 1642, Spanish authorities named him Bishop of Asunción.

Eventually, Cárdenas came into conflict with Governor Gregorio de Hinestrosa. Seeking popular support, he used public accusations against the Jesuits to build up power and prestige among the *encomenderos* (local leaders) of Asunción. When he attempted to force the closure of the Jesuit college in Asunción, he was expelled from the city.

In response, Cárdenas began a campaign against the Jesuits. He publicly accused them of enslaving Amerindians, of creating a secret government, and of running their own "kingdom" in the Alto Paraná River basin. He spread rumors that the Jesuits operated secret gold and diamond mines, that they withheld funds from the Church and the Crown, and that they grew rich, while the industries of their missions took laborers and markets away from Asunción's citizens.

Cárdenas's campaign against the Jesuits led the disgruntled citizens of Asunción to elect him as their governor in 1649. Cárdenas then raised an army to force the Jesuits out of Paraguay. Jesuit-trained Guaraní troops defeated Cárdenas's soldiers, however, and the bishop fled to exile in Bolivia. Cárdenas's campaign was not a total loss, though; it had fueled popular resentment against the Jesuits that did not fade. Fears of the Jesuits' power and virtual autonomy helped spark the Comunero Revolt (1717–1735) and later led the Spanish Crown to force the Order's expulsion from Spanish territories in 1767.

Spanish control and supervision. Although the Jesuits provided "donations" to political and military authorities in Asunción, they did not pay the taxes and duties that the Crown demanded from its private citizens. They did not even provide Spanish colonial officers with specific estimates of what their missions produced, what the missionaries sold, and to whom the missions marketed their goods.

Because of their efforts, their skill, and, most important, thanks to their control of a large and compliant labor force that cost them little to develop and maintain, the Jesuits dominated the market for yerba mate from the 1630s onward. With ample labor and land, the Jesuits expanded their operations into other productive activities. They became a leading provider of quebracho wood, and tannin, used for tanning leather, which they distilled from the wood. They expanded their ranches and became important providers of leather, meat, and animals for use in mining and transport. As the Jesuits grew their mercantile activities, Spanish settlers in Asunción, Buenos Aires, Córdoba, and other towns grew resentful. They could not compete with the Jesuits, who operated outside of the arbitrary economic borders that restricted Spanish subjects and those who worked for them. Each transaction by the missionaries cost the settlers and the Crown a chance to earn a profit.

More important, neophytes under Jesuit authority were not subject to the labor demands of the encomienda system. As the missions expanded, their success took away the key resource that allowed the elite in Asunción to produce and market their goods.

Residents of Asunción focused their anger against the missions on the Jesuit operations in their town. A faction within the city campaigned to expel all Jesuits from the town in 1649. When the town council issued an expulsion decree, the Jesuits initially complied. After leaving Asunción, they sent an appeal to the viceregal authorities in Lima.

The viceroy and his advisors sided with the Jesuits. When the settlers prevented a governor selected by the viceroy from taking office in Asunción, the governor gathered Guaraní troops from

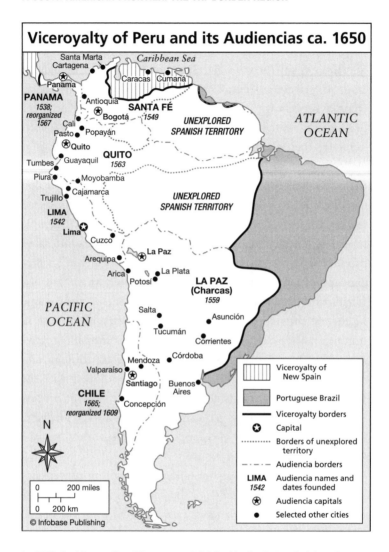

Viceroyalty of Peru and its Audiencias ca. 1650

In 1542, the Viceroyalty of Peru was established by Spain to administer its lands in South America. The viceroyalty was made up of six *audiencias*, or provincial administrations, including Charcas, in which the tri-border region town of Asunción became an important staging point for colonial expeditions to other parts of South America.

the missions and took the town by force. The Guaraní militia occupied the town for most of 1650.[24]

The services that the Jesuit missions provided for the Spanish

Crown made their position strong through the seventeenth century. The Guaraní militia allowed the Spanish to hold back Portuguese expansion throughout South America. In 1680, when Portuguese soldiers built a fort across the Río de la Plata from Buenos Aires, Spanish governors relied on Guaraní troops to increase their strength far beyond what the Portuguese could manage at the southern edge of their territory. Spanish and Guaraní soldiers destroyed the Portuguese settlement of Colônia do Sacramento.

When the settlers in Asunción rebelled again against Spanish authority in 1721, the missions provided troops and supplies to sustain the loyalist cause. This rebellion, which produced intermittent fighting from 1720 to 1735, was called the Comunero Revolt. Although nationalist historians in Paraguay regard the Comunero Revolt, or Commoners' Rebellion, as a precursor of the Independence Wars of the nineteenth century, the defense of Crown interests and the pacification of the territory was the last great service that the Jesuit missions provided to Spain. The Jesuits would continue to sponsor missions in other parts of South America, but the Order's fortune began to decline as a result of events outside their control.

The general mobilization of troops during the Comunero Revolt disrupted the agricultural and commercial operations that the missions depended on for their survival. In the wake of the revolt, famine plagued the mission lands. Disease and hardship led many of the neophytes to abandon the missions, and the declining population made the missions less profitable and less powerful.

Of greater concern were political changes within the colonial system. The Spanish Crown, united by the marriage and manipulations of Isabel and Ferdinand between 1469 and 1480, emerged as Europe's most powerful monarchy. The Habsburg line that inherited the united Crowns of Castile and Aragón expanded dramatically through the first half of the seventeenth century. The ambitions of Charles V and Philip II, however, left Spain bankrupt. The skills, energy, and ability of the monarchs who ruled the empire faded as the 1600s came to an end. The War of the Spanish Succession decided that a branch of the House of Bourbon would rule over Spain and its empire. After establishing themselves in Sevilla, the Bourbon kings worked to make their empire more efficient and their authority more effective.[25]

The relative autonomy of the Jesuits represented an important challenge to the Bourbon kings. The Jesuits no longer had the influence they once enjoyed within the viceregal government. Colonial administrators resented the economic powers of the Jesuits.

In 1750, the Treaty of Madrid gave the Portuguese Crown control of seven missions that operated along the southern banks of the Uruguay River. The transfer of the missions, and their lands and populations to Portuguese control, was part of a decade-long negotiation to settle the boundary between Portuguese and Spanish America from Guairá in the north to Uruguay and the Río de la Plata in the south. When notified of the treaty, the missionaries tried to move the neophytes to other missions. Guaraní leaders, unhappy with the proposed migration and enemies of the Portuguese, rallied thousands of the neophytes against the planned transfer. The Guaranís rose up against Spanish and Portuguese forces in 1754 and held out against grinding attacks until 1756.

The loss of these missions coincided with rising sentiment in Spain against the Jesuits. Although the Treaty of San Ildefonso returned the seven missions to Spanish control in 1761, the Crown did not allow the Jesuits to rebuild their operations. In 1767, it expelled the Jesuits from Spain and its colonies, which led to the end of all Jesuit operations in the Alto Paraná.[26]

The expulsion of the Jesuits did not turn back the changes that the Jesuits had brought to the region. The missions perfected the region's main industries and developed a labor force that served farms, ranches, and commercial activities across Spanish South America. The progress the Jesuits produced, however, ran counter to a growing desire in Spain and Portugal to extend and define their authority. The Jesuit enterprise did lead Spain and Portugal to revise their arbitrary definitions of borders that characterized their colonial possessions. The Jesuits were the only organization capable of forcing an effective redefinition of borders previously defined by material realities and social activities. The Jesuits' ambitions produced a new round of treaties and sparked a generation of rebellion. Their expulsion helped set in motion the collapse of the colonial system and a splintering of political authority that left the tri-border region part of no state for half a century.

5

From Colonies
to Republics

During the eighteenth century, Europe's interest in the tri-border region grew. The discovery of gold and diamonds in Mato Grosso caused speculators to rush in from the Brazilian coast and increased Portuguese supervision of the ill-defined boundaries between its American colonies and those of the Spanish. Although the Treaty of San Ildefonso ensured that Spain and Portugal would not go to war over the Río de la Plata and the Upper Paraná, Spanish authorities pushed to make their claims clear and more strongly defended. Finally, the Spanish expulsion of the Jesuits gave merchants between Asunción and Santa Fe (in present-day Argentina) hope that mercantile opportunities would finally develop in their favor.[27]

The arbitrary boundaries that Europeans had established in previous centuries had little influence over what actually happened locally. The settlers of the tri-border region set their own borders for their cultural, social, and material worlds. In the eighteenth century, political shifts in Spain promised a break from past practices. The Bourbon monarchy had taken control of Spain and its colonies, as a result of the settlements of the War of the Spanish Succession. After asserting its authority over potential rivals within Spain, the monarchy turned its attention to its American possessions. A series of reforms aimed to make the colonies more secure, better supervised, and more lucrative. In the tri-border region, these reforms came in 1776.[28]

To better supervise its South Atlantic possessions, the Bourbon monarchy formed the Viceroyalty of the Río de la Plata. The new area of governance encompassed Bolivia and Paraguay in the north and Argentina and the Banda Oriental in the south. The silver from Bolivia's mines that once entered the colonial trading system through Lima would now flow to Spain from Buenos Aires. What was once a colony of Asunción two centuries before now became the center of a revived Spanish authority in the Río de la Plata.

The Bourbon monarchy promised a number of changes that the citizens of the interior territories welcomed. First, it moved to tear down the administrative boundaries that did little to protect

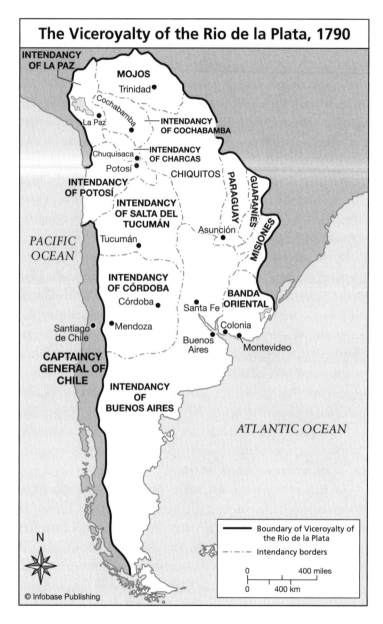

The Viceroyalty of the Río de la Plata was the last of Spain's South American viceroyalties. It was established in 1776 to defend the region of present-day Argentina, Bolivia, Paraguay, and Uruguay from British and Portuguese encroachment.

or advance the interests of the tri-border region. The Crown promised to lower restrictions on and charges against mercantile production and trade. The power of the merchants in coastal ports was reduced. Crown officials now allowed trade from any port in the Americas. Eventually, the producers of yerba mate and cotton in the Paraná River Basin would be able to trade with merchants in any port city in Spanish America legally and with few restrictions. Representatives of the Crown promoted local industries in an effort to make all parts of the realm productive. Increased production would increase the volume of trade to and from the Americas, which in turn would increase the revenue that imports and exports generated for Spanish merchants and the Crown.

In practice, the new administrative order upset life in the tri-border region in fundamental ways. The revived colonial system and structures created a more active and ambitious set of administrative and mercantile boundaries than before. Bureaucrats in Buenos Aires were much more active and much more demanding than those who had operated from Lima in earlier generations. At the same time, although the colonial system placed increased demands on the towns and resources of the Alto Paraná basin, the region still received less than its share of services. Military protection from indigenous raiders and bandeirantes remained inadequate. Local militias still provided the region's only secure defense. The reduced trade restrictions increased the amount of currency and encouraged expanded production in all the rural industries. Manufactured goods remained scarce and expensive, however, and the power of the merchants in Montevideo and Buenos Aires remained strong. Worse, the development of new cattle slaughtering and curing industries around the Río de la Plata estuary meant that ranching operations in the lands around the viceregal capital challenged those farther north, along the Paraguay and Alto Paraná rivers. As Buenos Aires changed from an isolated town into a dynamic capital city, the towns and settlements upriver grew resentful.

Of all the interior areas, the people who lived in the towns and settlements north of the Alto Paraná River came to hate the reforms the most. Two centuries had passed since the region helped rebuild Buenos Aires and the other towns along the lower Paraná. After 1776, the imposition of the new administrative order redirected the region's commerce away from the Andes and toward Buenos Aires. The commercial circles and relationships that had stood for centuries now lost most of their value. Colonial authority tried to force the flow of goods, labor, and services along new lines and within new borders. More important, energy and resources flowed out of the region. Little of value flowed toward the interior. A new generation of bureaucrats traveled to Asunción, but in a city of some 5,000 citizens (as registered in 1800), only 200 were of Spanish descent. These bureaucrats were officers who seldom performed their duties and whose main energies focused on escaping the region as soon as possible. In addition, after the expulsion of the Jesuits, the Alto Paraná River basin suffered from a near total lack of priests to serve the faithful. The situation was no better in Asunción: Although the Church made the city a bishopric after 1552, and 31 men were named to the post, it was vacant for 170 out of 262 years. A religious college provided a semblance of education for the city's residents, but it was chronically understaffed.

The overwhelming majority of the Spanish subjects living in Paraguay, estimated at more than 100,000, were scattered across the countryside in small settlements essentially unchanged since the sixteenth century. Few improved roads existed. Local authorities were from the regions they served as the sole representative of the Spanish Crown. Their local councils debated issues and met their needs with no help from Spain. Even the military remained a militia of mostly Guaraní troops.[29]

Nevertheless, Spain imposed a rigorous new order upon its American colonies. Events in Europe, however, suddenly severed transatlantic trade and communication.[30] The first disruption came as a result of the rebellion of Great Britain's North American colonies. The uprising pushed France and Great

Britain into war. As part of an effort to assert authority over its colonial subjects, the British navy imposed naval patrols and blockades that disrupted trade between continental Europe and the Americas. This disruption lasted less than five years.

The ensuing French Revolution created much greater problems. Great Britain enforced a blockade against France and its allies in 1792. With resources that far outstripped those of Spain, the government and navy of Great Britain asserted its global ambitions by establishing boundaries that isolated Spanish America from the non-Spanish world. Spain, France's unenthusiastic ally, found its shipping operations completely stalled. Then the situation worsened: As war between France and Great Britain continued, the blockade continued, and trade and communication between Spain and the Americas ceased. Merchants in the port cities along the Paraná and Paraguay rivers pushed to have regulations and restrictions on trade with foreigners lifted. Bureaucrats, still loyal to Spain but lacking clear instructions or even the funds necessary to fulfill their duties, became increasingly conservative, and tensions that separated the colonists from their Spanish overlords increased. The Bourbon monarchy's ambitious redefinition of the administrative and mercantile borders of its American colonies was paralyzed.

The arrival of a British expeditionary force in 1806 proved both troubling and revealing. The commander of the British force, Sir Home Popham, acted without orders. Diverting his naval and land forces from a successful invasion of South Africa, he hoped to separate South America from Spanish rule. The Spanish viceroy, the Marquis de Sobremonte, abandoned his post as British soldiers marched into Buenos Aires. Just as victory seemed assured, the citizens of the city formed a militia. They attacked the British troops and forced them back to their ships. When a second, larger force arrived in 1807, the citizen militia, reinforced by Guaraní soldiers and other troops from interior provinces, defeated the British a second time.[31]

The failure of Spanish authority set the viceroyalty on a path toward independence. Again, events in Europe served as a catalyst.

In 1807, Napoleon ordered the invasion of Iberia. He deposed the Bourbon king and named his elder brother, Joseph, as the new ruler of Spain and its colonies. Colonists across Spanish America declared their loyalty to the deposed order. In many cities, local councils asserted their right to rule in the place of the absent king.

The councils in Asunción and Buenos Aires were among the first to declare outright independence. On May 25, 1810, the town council in Buenos Aires asserted its authority over the lands the viceroy once ruled. News of the declarations in Buenos Aires quickly led councils in rival cities to assert their independence from Buenos Aires, as well as from Spain. The citizens of Asunción were some of the most strident opponents of Buenos Aires and its ambitions, and centuries of isolation had created a distinct identity in the city and the surrounding regions. Paraguay also lacked the factional strife that often plagued Buenos Aires. The city's governing council rallied behind the forceful leadership of José Rodríguez Gaspar de Francia. The son of a Spanish governor, Francia's education and experience prepared him to dominate council discussions. Asunción's citizens came to trust his judgment, and he provided a clear direction that put the territory's interests before all others. The fact that the territories north of the Alto Paraná River had maintained their own militias for generations also helped them organize an effective defense against the military challenges that soon came.[32]

Initially, negotiations between the representatives of the two cities led to a series of agreements that established a federation in the place of the viceroyalty. Radicals in Buenos Aires, however, pushed for firm control over all parts of the old colony, especially the agricultural lands of Paraguay and the mining districts of Bolivia. Manuel Belgrano commanded an expedition to the Alto Paraná in 1811. The local militia forces, which had time to prepare their defenses, defeated the invaders twice. Although the government in Buenos Aires continued to assert its claim to the region, the victories of 1811 left Paraguay autonomous.

After asserting its independence from Buenos Aires, Paraguay faced two challenges, one old and one new. Brazil had remained clear of the turmoil that independence produced in Spanish America, thanks to the flight of the Portuguese royal family from Portugal to Brazil in 1807. This action called into question the independence of the Portuguese Crown in relation to Great Britain, but it galvanized the Portuguese effort to assert its definition of borders and boundaries in South America. Portuguese armies considered the independence struggle in Spanish America as an opportunity to exercise control over frontier territories. Facing a much greater military threat from Brazil than ever before, the council in Asunción organized patrols and improved defenses along the Alto Paraná.

The rise of José Gervasio Artigas in Uruguay came to represent a more serious threat to Paraguay's independence. Artigas was part of an elite Uruguayan family. Comfortable in the merchant world of Montevideo, as well as in the countryside, where ranching expanded dramatically in the late eighteenth century, Artigas emerged as a champion of regional autonomy and of Amerindian rights. Artigas, like the citizens of Asunción, rebelled against Buenos Aires and its efforts to unify the old colony under its authority. He proposed the distribution of rural properties and the extension of greater political rights to Amerindians. Although he allied himself with federalist leaders in the territories between Buenos Aires and Paraguay, his movement threatened to tear down the lines that defined the cultural, social, and material worlds that colonial authorities had struggled to define.

To Asunción's leaders, Artigas was no friend. Although Asunción and Montevideo shared a common enemy, Artigas's proposed liberation of Amerindian peoples threatened to disrupt the labor systems that allowed Paraguay's elite to command and benefit from the labor of its rural workers. Initially, Artigas found himself in a difficult situation: his rebellion was taking place between the military forces of both Buenos Aires and Portuguese Brazil. Artigas tried to build a competitive trading system to rival Buenos Aires, and with Montevideo as its main

port, he promoted trade between cooperative European merchants and interior provinces along the Uruguay River. When
forces loyal to Artigas attacked Paraguayan patrols and ships,
Asunción launched attacks against Artigas's allies based south of
the Alto Paraná. Between 1816 and 1820, defeats and defections
reduced Artigas's army. Forced into exile, he was allowed by
Francia and the Paraguayan government to live out his life in
northern Paraguay.[33]

Although Paraguay's break from Buenos Aires was a clear
political victory, it hurt the region's economy. Paraguay was
unwilling to submit to Buenos Aires's authority and so found its
access to regional and foreign markets blocked by its rival.
Ranching and yerba mate production declined. Lack of customers eventually caused merchant houses in Asunción to close
their doors. The situation worsened after Spain's defeat, as foreign merchant ships traveled to Buenos Aires and Montevideo.
There, merchants traded the manufactured goods that they
brought with them from Europe for the leather, tallow, salted
beef, and silver that the locals offered in return. The commercial
revival that helped establish Buenos Aires as the mercantile center of the newly independent South America never reached the
Alto Paraná.

The Bourbon reformers hoped to establish a more rational
colonial system when they created the Viceroyalty of the Río de
la Plata. The reforms promoted changes that transformed the
Río de la Plata and Upper Paraná regions in material terms. The
impact of the reforms, however, worked against Spain's efforts to
consolidate its authority. When events in Europe in 1808 undermined the Bourbon Crown, and colonials moved to assert their
authority, the viceroyalty fell into political and military chaos.
Town councils, with distinct visions of a better future, first
declared autonomy and then independence from their European
overlords.

Immediately after these political changes took hold, the
underlying differences between Buenos Aires and the settlers in
the far north of the viceroyalty emerged. Resentments that had

built up over the centuries created in Asunción a strong and united group that commanded the loyalty of the population who lived and worked in Paraguay. When forces from Buenos

THE BOTANIST AND "*EL SUPREMO*"

One of the greatest adventures of the colonial era in South America was the tour of two men through Spain's colonies at the end of the eighteenth century. Aimé Jacques Alexandre Bonpland was a medical doctor, naturalist, and botanist, and Alexander von Humboldt, an expert in mining and political economy. Inspired by the ideals of the European "Enlightenment," as well as the wonders of the Americas, the two traveled, studied, documented, and then published their observations in a series of works that scholars continue to use to this day.

Afterward, Bonpland returned to South America, where he had obtained a professorial position in Buenos Aires. He resigned his post there, however, and instead renewed his explorations. His stated ambition was to study the production of yerba mate in the wild. In 1819, with the permission of officials in Entre Ríos Province, which then controlled the northeastern frontier of the United Provinces of the Río de la Plata, he crossed the Uruguay River and traveled north.

When Paraguayan authorities learned of his presence, Dr. José Rodríguez Gaspar de Francia, the dictator of the newly independent Paraguay (whom Paraguayans referred to as "El Supremo"), ordered Bonpland's arrest. Charged with spying, he was held prisoner on the grounds of an abandoned Jesuit mission. International leaders, including Simón Bolívar, begged for his release, but the dictator ignored their protests. Although "El Supremo" issued an official order ending his confinement in 1829, Bonpland remained in Paraguay until 1831.

After leaving Paraguay, Bonpland settled in Corrientes, an Argentine province located on Paraguay's southern border. The governor of Corrientes granted him an estate. He eventually moved to Santa Ana, in Uruguay, where he continued his research until his death in 1858. Bonpland's experience demonstrates the lengths to which Francia and his dictatorship would go to enforce the separation between Paraguay and the outside world. Bonpland's pursuit of scientific information counted for little. His violation of the borders that Francia and his supporters forced upon the tri-border region revealed the ambition and the arrogance of Francia for the world to see.

Aires tried to coerce their allegiance, the ability of the Paraguayans to act in common defense of their interests allowed them to break from all outside authority.

Spain never got the chance to challenge the independent forces in Paraguay: An expedition the Crown assembled to invade the Río de la Plata mutinied in 1820, which sparked a revolution that created a constitutional monarchy and a brief revival of liberal rule. The events in Spain demoralized the loyalists in the Americas. Subsequent military defeats in Chile and then Peru brought the end of Spanish rule in 1825.

Under Spanish rule, however, no clear boundaries were established that separated one newly declared country from its neighbors, and the independence struggle shattered the unity that had existed under colonial rule. The administrative and commercial systems that the Bourbon monarchy imposed on the Americas disintegrated even before the independence struggle reached its final phases. Further, the cultural and social borders that colonial practice and privilege defined became muddled, as international and local forces waged war against any traditions the colonial era had established. Spain's exit from South America left in its wake a number of urban centers with conflicting ambitions and claims in overlapping frontiers: each would try to impose its will in creating new boundaries, and each would face resistance from rival political centers and from the unwilling citizens who the authorities compelled to join their arbitrarily declared and loosely defined nations.

6

Nations
and
Boundaries

Paraguay's first leader after it achieved independence from Spain, José Gaspar Rodríguez de Francia, created the strongest state in South America by building on Paraguay's history and its geography. Its colonial experience was one of isolation, and the independence struggle had left Paraguay autonomous. By taking charge of the land and by organizing the labor of the country, Francia's dictatorship gathered what resources Paraguay possessed and built a relatively strong military and a centralized bureaucracy. The dictator's political allies in Paraguay, who formed an elite group that lived off the land and labor they commanded, lived in the shadow of the state. The majority of Paraguay's citizens knew little of the outside world. In essence, Francia established the most arbitrary borders in the history of the tri-border region. His nation was defined mainly by rejection of the outside world. Its independence was enforced but not achieved in actuality.[34]

That Paraguay existed as an independent country was clear. Exactly what territory it encompassed, however, was not. The dictatorship claimed lands to the north, east, and south that its neighbors also claimed. Francia's armies patrolled its "borders," and forts protected the key river approaches, but Paraguay's claims stood by default rather than proof. In fact, neither Argentina nor Brazil fully recognized Paraguay's right to exist. Although the *unitarios* (the political faction that tried to unite all of the Río de la Plata colonies) failed to retain control of power, the federalists proved to be more serious rivals. After 1829, Juan Manuel de Rosas, the leader of the federalist movement in Buenos Aires, became the region's most important military and political leader. He moved to put allies in charge of all the territories that were once part of the collapsed viceroyalty. For Rosas, Paraguay's autonomy was a potential threat.

Brazil challenged Paraguay's assertion of independence in two ways. First, it claimed Paraguayan land as its own and refused to recognize the legitimacy of the borders that Francia established and patrolled. Second, Brazil's rulers regarded Paraguay as a threat to their security. Although Francia pursued

Federalist leader Juan Manuel de Rosas became governor of Buenos Aires in 1829, a post he held until he was deposed in 1852. One of the first caudillos, or military dictators, in South America, Rosas was successful in unifying Argentina, due to his ability to identify with the common people.

a policy of isolation, Paraguay's existence as an independent, constitutionally defined state was a provocative example for the colonial subjects of Portugal. Paraguay's independent existence, in the opinion of the authorities in Rio de Janeiro, inspired independence movements in southern and western territories.

Military capability made these Argentine and Brazilian threats unimportant to Paraguay, which had defeated Argentina in its attempt to force a merger at the start of the independence era. Without a rival faction within Paraguay, Rosas and his fed-eralist allies could not challenge Francia's authority. Brazil pos-sessed a much greater military capability, which grew stronger as the decades passed. Geography, however, continued to check Brazilian ambitions. Although the colonial government in Rio de Janeiro may have wanted to challenge Paraguay, it lacked the ability to transport and maintain large numbers of troops in the region. No roads yet existed. No rail lines connecting Guairá, Mato Grosso, and the coastal cities had been built. The Brazilian army built forts along the banks of the Alto Paraná River but had trouble staffing and supplying them.

These conditions guaranteed Paraguayan independence. Those in charge in Rio de Janeiro or Buenos Aires might assert their authority over Paraguay, but their assertions fell before the challenge of Paraguay's military power and the vast distances that separated Paraguay from its coastal rivals. The isolation of Paraguay provided one effective boundary. The unique colonial experience of its settlers created an even firmer line of separa-tion. Brazil's imperial ambitions and the meddling of Argentine federalists had little impact on Paraguay's sovereignty. The col-lapse of colonial authority created an opportunity for anyone who could match political vision with the borders that tradi-tion, experience, and history had already established in the area. Francia made the most of this opportunity. Military vigilance and closed borders made Paraguay too strong and too isolated to challenge.[35]

Francia had created a political and military system that revolved around him. When he died on September 20, 1840, he left a political vacuum that no one in Paraguay was fully pre-pared to fill. Intrigues and plots swirled, as the favored few of Asunción's political class competed for power. Military interven-tion dictated a political solution, and Carlos Antonio López emerged as the leading figure. Working behind the scenes between 1841 and 1843, he became Paraguay's head of state in 1844. Once in possession of the state, he moved to centralize power and establish a new dictatorship.[36]

López built on what Francia had begun. He imposed changes that challenged the cultural, social, and material borders that had traditionally separated the rulers from the ruled in Paraguay. He continued to use the state as a machine to control the country: The government confiscated the land still in the hands of Amerindians, and it also nationalized the yerba mate industry. The government then organized the seized properties for more intensive exploitation. State farms and ranches provided a growing revenue stream that supported a relatively large military. Unlike Francia, López promoted limited innovations. He hired experts from abroad to create industries and slightly diversify the economy. He also allowed expanded foreign trade, although he maintained tight border controls.[37]

López made Paraguay's infrastructure stronger in two ways: He expanded the national police force and extended their operations to rural as well as urban areas. He also ordered the construction of roads that would allow the military to move over land faster than before. He established military bases in the Chaco and, for the first time, began the pacification of that territory. In the disputed south and west, López's more organized, better trained, and better equipped police and naval patrols made the country's border claims much more concrete. The lands south and east of the Alto Paraná River appeared to be securely under Paraguayan control, so López ordered his patrols to facilitate rather than block trade. Merchants found Paraguay's urban markets open, although trade was tightly regulated. The reasonable treatment of foreign merchants prevented any incidents that might have led to conflicts with neighbors or European governments. Consequently, although Paraguay seemed to be consolidating its hold on the land that Argentina and Uruguay also claimed, Paraguayan actions were not strong enough to mobilize protest or challenge.

Paraguay's rivals remained preoccupied with other conflicts. Argentina, for example, continued to be divided, as Juan Manuel de Rosas's policies only benefited his province of Buenos Aires. His most provocative policy involved foreign trade. Although Rosas was a federalist, he tried to force foreign merchants to trade exclusively in Buenos Aires, which would allow his government to capture tariff revenue that might otherwise benefit his rivals. His policies angered Argentines in the interior and foreign governments alike. Twice his government fell into war with Great Britain and France. By trying to put his province's interests before all others, Rosas spent his political and military resources. Therefore, although he remained in power through the 1840s, he lacked the forces and the ambition necessary to challenge Paraguay's interests.[38]

Rosas did contribute to Paraguay's success by meddling in the politics of the Corrientes Province. At the start of the independence era, the *caudillos* (military dictators) in Corrientes claimed the Jesuit lands as their territory. The militia cavalry of Corrientes, however, was no match for Paraguay's, and Francia was able to repossess what remained of the Jesuit missions as state lands. In the 1830s, as Paraguay consolidated its power and extended its control over the disputed lands between the Uruguay and Alto Paraná rivers, federalists and unitarios fell into battle in Corrientes. Rosas offered and withdrew support for a string of caudillos in Corrientes as the decades passed. The enemies of Rosas turned to Paraguay for support. The Francia dictatorship refused any involvement, but after Francia's death, negotiations began and resulted in an agreement, which was signed in 1841. It settled all border claims between the two regions and proposed joint patrols and regulation of the Paraná and Paraguay rivers, and any foreign trade that was carried out there.

Had the unitarios held on to power in Corrientes, Paraguay might have secured more lucrative contracts with foreign traders for their exports and might have been able to import what foreign goods its government deemed desirable with fewer restraints. Its military concerns along its southern frontier would have lessened, and its government might have challenged Brazil more aggressively. The collapse of the unitario government in Corrientes in 1845, however, made all such agreements useless. López continued to challenge Rosas and his federalist allies. In 1849 and again in 1851, Paraguay invaded Corrientes.

Although it achieved some success, the presence of supporting forces from Entre Ríos Province turned back the Paraguayan army. Before the pro-Rosas forces could mount a threat, though, their commanders turned against each other. This left Paraguay's definition of its political boundaries intact by default.[39]

Brazil continued to regard Paraguay as a rival and a threat, but by 1840 it viewed the Rosas dictatorship as a greater problem. Brazilian policy makers believed that joint maintenance of Paraguay by Brazil and Argentina would prevent war. Brazil offered to recognize Paraguay's independence and sovereignty in 1844; however, disputed borderlands remained a problem. Although López quickly approved the proposed treaty, the government in Rio de Janeiro objected to the boundary lines the treaty declared along the Alto Paraná River. In 1845, after months of issuing no declaration, Brazil informed Paraguay that the treaty was unacceptable. Brazilian authorities had no reason to move quickly. The territory in question remained as isolated from its political and economic centers as before. For Paraguay, the lines declared in the treaty ratified both the political and geographical ambitions of the López dictatorship and the cultural and material worlds of the Paraguayans who lived and worked there. The rich yerba mate and quebracho forests remained the mainstay of Paraguay's commercial empire. Both sides moved military forces to the disputed border regions and built forts that reinforced their claims. No serious clashes occurred, however. Brazil eventually decided to ignore the border issue and settle its relations with Paraguay. In 1851, the two countries ratified an amended version of the treaty, with provisions for mutual defense against Argentine military actions.[40]

In 1852, Juan Manuel de Rosas fell from power. This ended the threat to Paraguay's territorial ambitions in the south. It also allowed free trade up the Paraná and Paraguay rivers for the first time. The López dictatorship hoped to capitalize on these opportunities. Trade increased, foreign experts traveled into Paraguay in greater numbers, and the dictatorship took its first steps toward a thorough modernization of its military: European officers provided training, foreign guns and ships were used to equip Paraguay's militia and navy, and the government built the foundation of a domestic armaments industry. By the 1860s, Paraguay produced its own ships and foundries, which accelerated the modernization of its naval squadrons and river defenses.[41]

Paraguay's confidence led to stronger assertions of its ambitions. It placed firmer regulations on foreign trade and patrolled disputed territories over land and on river more aggressively. As Paraguay's efforts to set boundaries gained strength, the country faced a new round of challenges from overseas. British, French, and American merchants were all united in a desire for free and unfettered commerce in all South American markets. They wanted to build commercial links that drew Paraguay into their commercial world. Their competition for access to the products that Paraguayans produced directly challenged the arbitrary lines of power and authority that the López dictatorship established. The dictatorship's tariffs and inspections, while an improvement over the forced isolation of the Francia era, interfered with the pursuits of market and profit. Ambassadors pushed to have the restrictions removed. The dictatorship ignored all requests. By the 1860s, the failed promise of open3trade left Paraguay diplomatically isolated.[42]

Brazil, on the other hand, was freed from the threat that the Rosas dictatorship in Buenos Aires Province once presented, and it had little tolerance for Paraguay's ambitions. The newly constituted Argentine Confederation dropped all disputes with Brazil and applied new pressure on Paraguay over the disputed lands in Corrientes and Misiones. The death of Carlos Antonio López on September 10, 1862, left Paraguay in the hands of his heir, Francisco Solano López. Lacking any skill in diplomacy and overly confident that Paraguay's military capabilities surpassed all its neighbors, Solano López allowed the country's complex string of border disputes to escalate into war.

Believing that an intervention in a final dispute between members of the Blanco and Colorado parties over Uruguay's political future would allow Paraguay to assert its rights to all the land it claimed, Paraguayan soldiers crossed into Corrientes in 1865 and marched south. The incursion led to a declaration of war against Paraguay by Argentina, Brazil, and Uruguay. Initial battles made it clear that Paraguay's forces weren't superior to those of its rivals; a disastrous naval battle on the Riachuelo River destroyed most of Paraguay's navy and left the country open to invasion. Incompetence and poor preparations on the part of Argentina and Brazil at first delayed Paraguay's inevitable defeat. However, when the allied forces of Paraguay's enemies completed their invasion, observers estimated that the war had cost it two-thirds of its population.[43]

The War of the Triple Alliance completely reversed the trends

THE DICTATOR'S CONSORT: ELISA ALICIA LYNCH

José Gaspar Rodríguez de Francia established and enforced rigid control of Paraguay's asserted borders during his dictatorship. Unlike the "El Supremo" dictatorship, however, during the López era, select foreigners were invited to conduct trade and develop targeted industries within the isolated country.

Elisa Lynch personified this shift in a unique—even romantic—fashion. Born in Ireland, Lynch met Francisco Solano López in Paris, during a tour of Europe. López convinced Lynch to travel with him back to Paraguay. Despite her prior marriage and López's public relationship with Juana Pesoa, his common-law wife, Lynch became Paraguay's de-facto first lady and the center of Paraguay's revived high society after 1862. López built "Madame Lynch" a personal palace and held state dinners and galas there during his brief reign. Her presence and influence introduced Paraguay to European manners and styles.

Lynch accompanied López through the bitter end of the War of the Triple Alliance. Then, forced into exile, she struggled for the rest of her life to reclaim what remained of the López estate. After her death in Paris in 1886, Lynch's story was recast in European novels and plays. In the 1950s, President Alfredo Stroessner recognized her as a national heroine. In 1964, her remains were returned to Paraguay, where they were buried in the National Pantheon of Heroes, the national cemetery in Asunción.

In 1862, Francisco Solano López succeeded his father, Carlos Antonio López, as president of Paraguay. Lacking diplomatic skills, Solano López ill-fatedly led his country into war against Argentina, Brazil, and Uruguay, in 1864. Known as the War of the Triple Alliance, this conflict was the bloodiest in Latin American history—more than half of Paraguay's people were killed and some 55,000 square miles of the nation's territory were annexed by Brazil and Argentina.

in the tri-border region. Although three countries carried conflicting claims over the region until 1865, only Paraguay had managed to build roads and forts and mount naval patrols that effectively promoted its sovereign claims. State support of farming and ranching and its consolidation of the yerba mate industry incorporated the region fully into Paraguay's centralized and closely controlled economy. The promotion of trade across the docks of Itapúa dramatically increased travel and trade along the Alto Paraná River. The government's restrictions on foreigners and its ban on foreign ownership of land also left the territory open to only Paraguayan citizens and their concerns.

The challenge of war forced Brazil and Argentina to make good their claims on the land. Both began by modernizing and expanding their military forces. They built communication and transportation lines into the region that helped to effectively extend their authority there for the first time. As the battles destroyed Paraguay's ships and forts, the allied armies pushed back Paraguay's nominal control over the area. At the war's end, Paraguay's survival seemed doubtful. Its claims over the tri-border region and other disputed lands came to an end.

Argentina became the dominant force in the region after 1870. Brazil had destroyed the Paraguayan threat and had consolidated its claims on the Alto Paraná River basin, but the region still was too far from the coast to be of much value to investors and speculators. A booming coffee industry, centered hundreds of miles east of Guairá, in São Paulo, became the focus of Brazil's economic expansion. Argentine officials reacted differently to Paraguay's defeat. Politicians became concerned over the country's lack of authority along its borders. With an expanded and modernized military in the war's wake, the Argentine government launched military expeditions against all remaining pockets of local autonomy. The federal government asserted its control over its northern frontier. It mapped its border and took possession of unoccupied lands. Argentine companies and capital poured into the tri-border region; many had ambitions to modernize and develop the area's rural industries and expand its commerce. For the locals who survived the destruction of war, Argentina's move to redefine the area's economic and political lines represented nothing short of an invasion.

7

The World Comes to Paraguay

Between 1870 and 1930, Argentina took the lead in developing the tri-border region. Misiones, Itapúa, Alto Paraná, and Guairá—the Argentine, Paraguayan, and Brazilian territories that jointly formed the tri-border region—had been swept clear of the settlements, farms, and ranches that Paraguay's nationalistic dictatorships had organized and directed from Asunción. The territory had value, thanks to what remained of the Jesuit properties from the eighteenth century. The War of the Triple Alliance, however, had stripped the area of the laboring population that collected and prepared the yerba mate, herded the cattle, and cut the lumber from the forests.

Consequently, the process of reclaiming the tri-border region required resources: foreign investment, hired labor, and entrepreneurial leadership. This came with an alliance of Argentine and international initiative. The Argentine government and Argentine companies, backed by British and other foreign investors, rebuilt ports and roads, revived old activities, and developed new industries. The land that had been left to mestizo settlers and surviving Guaraní villages gained commercial value. Private companies took control of land that had before been open to free transit. Paraguayans now found themselves as tenants or trespassers on the land of their fathers.

Paraguay, so damaged by war, benefited from the redevelopment of the tri-border region. The reconstructed national government that arose in the place of the Solano López dictatorship leased and sold land to raise funds and pay its debts. The survivors of the war returned to the region and found work. Redevelopment shattered what boundaries remained after the war. The process of development transformed southeastern Paraguay into an international zone. Foreigners assigned value, defined order, and commanded labor that they used to expand ranching and farming industries they now controlled. In turn, the arbitrary political ambitions of past generations evaporated. The Paraguay that almost was, simply ceased to be.[44]

Argentina was initially content to establish its border claims and foster development in Corrientes and Misiones. Past history

BOLIVIA'S LOST COASTAL LANDS

Unlike Paraguay, Bolivia controlled a number of important ports on the Pacific coast of South America at the end of the independence era. These ports connected Bolivia directly to the world market and allowed its leaders to develop the country's economy through the promotion of industries specializing in exports. However, the physical and economic damage of the Independence Wars made it difficult for Bolivia to revive its mining industries, which had once been the foundation of its economy. In the middle of the nineteenth century, its leaders relied on foreign companies, most based in Great Britain or Chile, to direct the recovery efforts.

Bolivia achieved some success with its nitrate industry. In the Atacama Desert region, located south of Peru on the Pacific coast, foreign companies mined rich nitrate deposits and processed them into fertilizer and other products. Economic and political problems, however, led the Bolivian government to raise taxes and place other regulatory restrictions on the foreign mining companies that operated in the region. Bolivian leaders hoped to increase public revenues, but these moves angered Chilean companies, workers, and investors, who thought the territory should have become part of Chile during the independence era.

A crisis began in 1878, when the Antofagasta Nitrate & Railway Company refused to pay taxes charged by the Bolivian government on its operations. Bolivia declared the company in foreclosure and, in the face of threats from the Chilean government, moved to auction the company's assets. In response to the Bolivian government's actions, on February 14, 1879, the Chilean army moved to occupy the port city of Antofagasta. Bolivia declared war. When Chile rejected Peru's attempt to negotiate a settlement, the Peruvian government opted to ally with Bolivia against its southern aggressor.

Chile's armed forces were superior in all respects to those of the allies, and it quickly won a series of land and naval battles that consolidated its control of the disputed territory. It invaded Peru and captured Lima in January 1881. Although the Peruvian army collapsed, the Chilean conquest of Peru continued until October 20, 1883. The Treaty of Ancón left Chile in control of Antofagasta, as well as the Peruvian port of Arica. Stripped of its access to the ocean, Bolivia was forced to rely on rivers for its foreign trade, as had Paraguay, since its founding in the colonial period.

made the Argentine government anxious to put its hold on Misiones beyond challenge. Although official recognition of the borderline would not come until 1876, Argentine President Domingo Faustino Sarmiento proposed the inclusion of the region in his national land colonization plan in 1869. However, the national government's intentions concerned leaders in Corrientes who hoped to secure Misiones as part of their province. Corrientes issued land deeds to anyone who was willing to settle in Misiones.

Although the land (suitable for harvesting yerba mate and quebracho wood from preexisting forests) had potential, geography presented important barriers to any attempts to colonize it. Overland trails existed, but they were nearly impassible in wet weather. The Paraná River was navigable, but the Uruguay was too shallow for all but the smallest boats. Consequently, land located any significant distance from the Alto Paraná River was difficult to exploit without ample labor and the creation of new trails and roads.[45]

Settlers from Corrientes and Entre Ríos did move into Misiones, but most focused on forestry activities. The Corrientes provincial government discouraged the revival of yerba mate harvesting by imposing special taxes on the product if produced in the newly opened territory. Hoping to settle the land with farmers who would pioneer the expansion of new crops, in 1875, the Corrientes government passed a law that granted up to 2.3 square miles (6 square kilometers) of land to individuals or companies that agreed to develop towns and farmlands on the sites of abandoned missions. One attempt was made in 1876 near the Loreto mission, just inside the Misiones border. Poor transportation, a lack of capital, and a devastating flood forced the European settlers who had signed on with the experiment to abandon their lots within a year of their arrival.[46]

Despite this failure, in the months that followed, provincial and national governments competed to colonize and claim Misiones. The movement of settlers into the region would help political leaders realize their dreams of a better future. In some respects, provincial and national authorities viewed the destruction that the War of the Triple Alliance caused as an opportunity. Policy makers regarded Amerindians and their descendants as inferior, uncultured people who stood in the way of progress. This view, most actively promoted by Argentine presidents Bartolomé Mitre and Domingo Faustino Sarmiento, promoted settlement by Europeans, regarded as progressive and racially superior, as a way to bring progress to unsettled lands. By clearing out the less cultured and less capable American-born populations, the war, in their perverse view, accelerated the "civilizing" of the tri-border region.[47]

As the years passed, the governments of Corrientes and Argentina sought additional contracts with foreign colonization companies. Both focused on private companies that recruited colonists in Europe. Provincial authorities approved 10 private colonies. All took up land near old missions at the southwestern end of Misiones.[48]

Provincial authorities continued to claim Misiones as part of its territory, however. Initially, they did not offer land to any colonization projects in the territory that was once claimed by Paraguay. The provincial government believed that settling these eastern districts would lead to rapid deforestation and the destruction of the wild supplies of yerba mate and quebracho wood. In the 1860s, these authorities passed laws that prevented land sales and prohibited settlement in all unincorporated districts of the territory. By banning settlement, they hoped to preserve sufficient stands of both trees for the future. Locals who needed land to support their families ignored the government's arbitrary boundaries. An estimated 1,800 migrant families moved into the region and exploited it as best they could. Having to rely on the rivers to transport their goods, few found commercial success. Most lived in crude huts and relied on fishing and farming for their survival.[49]

The Argentine government finally nationalized Misiones in 1881. Recognizing that its authority over the territory had come to an end, the provincial government sold title to large tracts of land in eastern Misiones to speculators. The national government ignored the sales and continued to rely on private companies and European settlers to fill up the territory's empty lands. The process was slow, particularly in the east. By 1900, only 12 new colonies had been created, and all were in Misiones' southwestern corner.[50]

Brazil made significant improvements in the transportation links that connected the tri-border region to the Atlantic coast during and immediately after the War of the Triple Alliance. Its influence in the region, however, remained slight. After defeating Paraguay, Brazil maintained its frontier forts and military patrols. Unlike Argentina, no attempt was made to settle the region. Brazil's position was shaped by two factors.

First, the distance between the Atlantic and the Alto Paraná was too great to attract individual colonists or private companies who might have settled the land. Those who did come to the region focused on logging. Because of this concentration, the forest established the boundary for settlement and development. The forest's density meant that from 1870 to 1930, the line of settlement remained far to the east of the tri-border region. The companies that controlled the logging resources, by purchasing or leasing the land, actually used private guards and patrols to prevent squatters from settling the land.[51]

Second, the imperial government of Brazil clouded property rights with its actions in the wake of the War of the Triple Alliance. Although the war ended Paraguay's challenge to Brazil's borders, the Brazilian government remained concerned over the integrity and security of the land along the banks of the Alto Paraná. It had declared in 1850 that all unoccupied property in frontier territories was property of the state. When it pushed the scattered Paraguayan settlements out of the tri-border region, however, it did nothing to promote the settlement of the area by Brazilian colonists.[52] The imperial government distributed grants of large tracts of public land in its interior territories, but it did so only to encourage the construction of rail lines and roads.

Although colonization in the tri-border region progressed slowly before 1914, some development of the area did occur. Initially, the focus of economic development was in Paraguay. The government had no resources with which it might fund the reconstruction of the country after 1870. It secured foreign loans, but sluggish trade and the devastation that the War of the Triple Alliance had caused made it impossible for the Paraguayan government to service its debt. To avoid financial disaster, the Paraguayan government sold off much of its public lands.[53]

To simplify the process, the government sold the public lands in large lots. Some land sold for as little as 100 pesos per square league, but most Paraguayans lacked the cash necessary for even the least expensive purchase. The lack of a banking or credit system capable of providing mortgages for individuals meant that almost all the land sold went to foreign individuals and companies.[54]

Argentine investors bought control of ranching, timber, and yerba mate tracts in the southern districts. La Industrial, a British company, purchased lands along the Alto Paraná and became the largest collector and processor of yerba mate in the country. International Products, based in the United States, bought up ranch lands and built slaughterhouses and packing plants near Asunción. Soon, it was a major producer of corned beef for the North American and European markets. By 1930, 19 foreign companies controlled half of Paraguay's land.[55]

Although foreign companies took control of lands that had once been owned by the state, the investment boom had some positive effects. Population grew rapidly. In 1872, the Paraguayan government recorded 231,000 persons in the country's first national census. In 1899, the census total reached 635,000. Although the statistics are not reliable, the scale accurately reflects the trend. Immigration into the country (mostly of Paraguayan exiles and new arrivals from neighboring countries) accounted for most of the growth.[56]

Trade also rebounded, thanks to foreign investment and the

shipment of goods and raw materials out of the country. Between 1880 and 1900, the volume of exports and imports increased fivefold. Although Paraguay remained politically unstable, economic recovery continued until 1914. Foreign investors helped build a national banking system that served both the government and private investors. The government and foreign companies helped repair and extend the country's railroads. Public and private investment also expanded and modernized ports along the Paraguay and Paraná rivers.[57]

By 1914, Paraguay's political leaders hoped that the country was on a path of sustained recovery. World War I, which created a strong demand for Paraguayan ranch products, maintained these hopes. When the war ended, however, international conditions turned against the country. Paraguay's beef and leather lost their market shares, and international prices collapsed. In the 1920s, the development of a synthetic tanning process destroyed the market for natural tannin, which is produced from quebracho wood. Foreign capital became scarce and investments declined. Even the market for yerba mate shrunk, as a result of increased Brazilian production and a subsequent fall in prices.[58]

These conditions hit the tri-border region hard. The government and the merchants in Paraguay had an especially difficult time. Economic conditions encouraged political turmoil, as political factions fought for control of the state and its resources. A partial recovery seemed underway by the late 1920s, but the Great Depression plunged Paraguay's commercial industries into crisis. Fortunately, for the majority of Paraguay's citizens, the Great Depression seemed to begin and end in Asunción. Although opportunities for wage work became scarce, most Paraguayans lived in the countryside and had access to land. They could devote themselves to subsistence agriculture and wait for better times.[59]

In the midst of this cycle of economic and political crises, on Paraguay's western border, Bolivia pressed its claim to own Chaco lands that had traditionally been considered part of Paraguay. The discovery of oil and the aggressive efforts of

In the late 1920s, the Bolivian army entered the Chaco region of Paraguay with the purpose of annexing a strip of land that would give them access to the Pacific Ocean. This conflict—known as the Chaco War—was fought from 1932 to 1935, and despite enjoying a sizeable advantage in troop strength, the Bolivian army was defeated by Paraguay. Pictured here are Paraguayan troops passing by a recently constructed bridge built along the Chaco warfront.

U.S.–based Standard Oil to develop the fields had made the alignment of borders in the Chaco desert an important issue. The Bolivian government occupied increasing chunks of territory after 1904.

Although Bolivia's actions provoked Paraguayan nationalists, the government in Asunción turned to international arbitration to settle each dispute. The memory of the costs of the War of the Triple Alliance made a military confrontation unthinkable. Despite Paraguayan concessions, however, Bolivia increased its demands, and skirmishes between the two armies along the frontier between 1931 and 1932 led to war.

The Bolivians anticipated a quick victory. Their army was almost double the size of Paraguay's, and it possessed better equipment. German advisors helped the Bolivian officer corps plan and execute the first offensive. Surprisingly, the Paraguayan government mobilized its resources quickly and effectively. The Paraguayan army relied on a defensive barrier of trenches and forts. The attacks directed at the defensive works between 1932 and 1933 destroyed the spirit of the Bolivian invaders. Paraguay capitalized on its success by launching offensive operations that all but cleared the Chaco of Bolivian troops. Bolivia lost an estimated 60,000 troops by the war's end in 1935. Paraguay lost 30,000.

The Great Depression and the Chaco War financially exhausted the Paraguayan government. The Great Depression also undermined Argentine efforts to colonize and develop the tri-border region. Private development of the yerba mate forests withered, and Brazilian operations located in Mato Grosso far north of the tri-border region gained market share, thanks to government support and trade concessions that Argentina made in order to preserve the Brazilian market for its grain exports. The Argentine government's programs to support sugar and tea production in Salta, La Rioja, and other Andean provinces also undermined competing plantations in Misiones.[60]

By the end of the 1930s, the tri-border region was again isolated and stagnant. Argentina's push to remake Paraguay had stalled, but the commercially driven development of the tri-border region partially filled the void created by the War of the Triple Alliance. New business ventures, the transport of labor and capital, and the revival of farming, ranching, and forestry stopped far short of revolution. When the Great Depression hit, the people who came to work in the area took control of the land and made it their own. Many who had worked on the ranches and plantations squatted on land and farmed for their own subsistence. Others, unable or unwilling to find land to support themselves and their families, moved south to the urban markets of Santa Fe, Córdoba, and Buenos Aires in Argentina, and Montevideo in Uruguay.

In the decades that followed, a new set of arbitrary boundaries and connections would appear. Political changes in Paraguay would lead to important shifts that would cause the tri-border region to become the center of the country's economic growth. In turn, conditions within Paraguay and abroad would make the region attractive to immigrants, who would fuel a population explosion in the region that continues today.

8

The *Stronato*

The Great Depression and the Chaco War emboldened the military and the veterans who pushed for political reforms. For 12 years, political factions backed by the military tried to dominate the country. In 1947, elections ended the Liberal Party's hold on power. The opposition Colorado Party took control. Imposing its own version of authoritarian rule, Colorado leaders returned to the question of Paraguay's future.[61]

The figure who would drive the debate was Alfredo Stroessner. Stroessner entered the Military School of Asunción at age 16, and by 1947, just months before his thirty-fifth birthday, he had risen to the rank of Lieutenant-Colonel. His connections to the Colorado Party aided his military career. In 1951, he became commander-in-chief of the Paraguayan armed forces. Stroessner developed important supporters in the Colorado Party and the military. His ambition led him to isolate and push from power a series of political rivals. By 1954, after toppling the sitting president, he orchestrated elections that put him in charge of the country. It was the first of seven electoral exercises that eventually allowed him to become the longest-ruling dictator in Latin America during the twentieth century. Secure in his position, Stroessner moved to strengthen the state. Police and military forces grew, as did their responsibilities for maintaining the country's security. The need for security pushed the dictatorship to find new sources of revenue. As a consequence of his regime's policy shifts, the tri-border region experienced significant changes.

Paraguay still faced its traditional challenges. Its largest neighbors, Brazil and Argentina, had enormous influence over the country's economic future. Since World War I, both countries had developed yerba mate and quebracho industries that competed with Paraguay's main export industries. Efforts to develop new agricultural, ranching, or commercial ventures would put Paraguay into competition with better-funded Argentine or Brazilian operations that had better access to markets and significant competitive advantages. The Stroessner regime at first worked to avoid conflict. Paraguay cooperated with the military and civilian governments that rotated in and out of power in

Alfredo Stroessner, who served as president of Paraguay from 1954 to 1989, was the longest-ruling dictator in Latin America during the twentieth century. Although Stroessner was responsible for stabilizing the country's currency, promoting new commercial agricultural industries, and building new schools, he spent half of Paraguay's income on establishing a strong military.

Argentina and set aside any discussion of past border disputes. This calm approach kept rail and river trade routes through Argentina to the Atlantic open and helped maintain Paraguay's traditional farming and ranching activities.

The dictatorship also pushed the development of a new source of revenue: state-sanctioned smuggling. The tri-border region became the key center in Paraguay's contraband trade. In 1957, the government sponsored the creation of a new city, Puerto Stroessner. Renamed Ciudad del Este in 1989, Puerto

Stroessner's location was its main attraction. It sat in the heart of the tri-border region, across the Alto Paraná River from Brazil and Argentina. The city was advertised as a tourist center. Iguazú Falls lay close by, and Salto del Guairá, one of the earliest colonial settlements in Paraguay, is just to the north. The construction of hotels and other tourist amenities did allow an increase in tourism, but the city's main industry quickly became the movement of goods across the Triple Frontier, free from inspections and taxes.

The smuggling operations involved a variety of products. Which products were smuggled where depended on the efforts of Argentina, Brazil, and other neighboring countries to use tariffs and other taxes as a means of creating boundaries around their national economies. The existence of different levels of taxes on liquor and tobacco products made the shipment of alcohol or cigarettes from a country with low taxes to a neighboring country that imposed higher duties a surprisingly profitable enterprise. The military, with the knowledge and approval of the dictator, used transport planes and trucks to move the merchandise and capture its cut of the profits. Puerto Stroessner also became a dumping ground for stolen cars and trucks that thieves drove across the Argentine or Brazilian border. A change of license plates made it easy to discard in Argentina vehicles stolen from Brazil or those stolen from Argentina in Brazil.[62]

For the first time in its long history, the tri-border region's isolation and its traditional lack of clear borders served the Paraguayan government's interests. Although Argentina and Brazil had passed laws and granted concessions to settle the area and develop the regional economy, in the 1950s, the Triple Frontier was still sparsely populated. Although forts and military patrols advertised the location of the official borders, residents in all three countries passed though what security systems existed with little trouble or delay. The rivers and forests of the region gave those with something to hide numerous ways to cross from one country into another and back again. Argentine and Brazilian authorities publicly asserted their authority over the lines that war and treaties had set, but the Stroessner regime gained profits by subverting the arbitrary borders that Paraguay's neighbors had imposed.

Stroessner also pushed for the development of the legal economy. The dictatorship invested heavily in infrastructure: New roads connected the tri-border region with Asunción and other urban centers, and the government built new schools, modernized its ports, and updated its utility systems. Borrowing funds from international creditors, the dictatorship funded new commercial ventures that would produce tax and tariff revenue to service the public debt. Working with private investors, Stroessner's regime promoted new commercial agricultural industries. With the rural population in central and southwestern Paraguay centered on producing food, this promotion of commercial agriculture focused on the departments of Itapúa and Alto Paraná. By the 1970s, agricultural exports surged: Paraguay became a major producer of soybeans, and investments in mechanization on larger farms helped revive the cotton industry.[63]

Continued growth required better access to wider markets. For Paraguay, this meant a need for improved relations with Brazil. However, border issues still caused tension between the two governments. For example, in the 1950s, as Stroessner consolidated his power, Brazil pressed its claims over Guairá Falls. On the other hand, the Brazilian government had begun its own push to develop the tri-border region, and a key part of any plan to exploit the Guairá was energy. Hoping to develop hydroelectric projects on the Alto Paraná, Brazil pressed for full sovereignty over what it regarded as a promising site to build a dam.

In the late 1950s, Brazil built new military bases and increased military patrols in the region. In 1962, it made public its ambitions to take control and develop Guairá Falls. In contrast to the events a century before, the Brazilian assertions led to negotiations. In 1964, Paraguay and Brazil announced plans to study and jointly develop the hydroelectric potential of the Alto Paraná River. The negotiations eventually led to two

The Itaipú Dam, located on the Upper Paraná River, on the Paraguay-Brazil border, includes the world's largest hydroelectric power plant. Brazil and Paraguay each own half of the dam, which supplies 25 percent of Brazil's consumed power and 90 percent of Paraguay's.

agreements. The Treaty of Ygauzu, signed in secret in 1966, recognized Brazil's rights to Guairá Falls. It also committed the two countries to a joint development of a hydroelectric project, with both sharing equally the electricity that the project would one day produce. A final concession ended a ban against the sale of land to foreigners along Paraguay's eastern border. This opened up Paraguay's part of the tri-border region to Brazilian companies and settlers. The agreement was made public when Paraguay and Brazil signed the Itaipú Treaty in 1973, which set out the details of the construction of Itaipú Dam. Although the construction took more than 16 years, the Paraguayan government received royalties from electricity sales beginning in 1983. The project attracted migrants who moved into the tri-border region in search of work. Puerto Stroessner, which was home to 49,423 residents in 1982, grew dramatically: By 1992, it grew to 133,881; a decade later, the population reached 233,350.

Just as the promotion of smuggling called into question the existence of Paraguay's authority over its political borders, these treaties and shared projects challenged the geographic, economic, and social boundaries that separated Brazil and Paraguay. The recognition of Brazilian authority over Guairá Falls reversed the stand over territory and sovereignty that led to the War of the Triple Alliance. The agreement to develop hydroelectric projects would fuel the expansion of Brazilian industries and encourage the settlement of the region by Brazilians. The influx of Brazilians would flood the region with a growing population that owed no loyalty to Paraguay and push Paraguayan citizens off the land.

Despite public and private efforts to promote economic development, smuggling remained the central occupation of the tri-border region. As contraband trade developed, the Brazilian city of Foz do Iguaçú expanded at a pace similar to that of Ciudad del Este. The illegal drug trade became an important part of cross-border commerce. In the 1960s, the transport of heroin from its Asian sources to the United States developed in the region. In the 1970s, tri-border dealers coordinated the transport of locally grown marijuana to Brazil, the United States, and Europe. In the 1980s, the tri-border region developed ties with the Colombia-based cocaine trade.[64]

Both the government and those who helped move the goods through the country profited from the drug-smuggling trade. The bribes and payoffs were part of a system of graft and corruption that helped Stroessner stay in power. Paraguay's involvement in drug smuggling angered officials in the United States who were aware of Paraguay's role and of the involvement of high government officials and the military in the drug trade. Despite public condemnation, the Stroessner regime grew less concerned with the opinion of the United States as the profits generated by drug running grew.[65]

The drug trade promoted the growth of money laundering in Puerto Stroessner and Foz do Iguaçú. Exchange houses, nominally in operation to help tourists convert their currencies, funneled cash from criminal organizations to banks outside the continent. Investigators estimate that money-laundering operations in the tri-border region in 2000 involved transactions worth $25 billion. The drug trade also encouraged the transportation of shipments of guns and ammunition through Paraguay into Brazil, in support of the gangs that controlled drug sales in São Paulo, Rio de Janeiro, and other large cities.[66]

DRUG SMUGGLING: THE CASE OF GENERAL ANDRÉS RODRÍGUEZ PEDOTTI

Paraguay's sluggish economic growth has encouraged smuggling of a wide range of products since the colonial era. When Alfredo Stroessner promoted the development of the tri-border region, smuggling activities expanded dramatically, with the clear approval of public authorities. In particular, drug smuggling became a major source of revenue for high-ranking government officials after 1960.

Although not a typical case, the record of General Andrés Rodríguez Pedotti illustrates the official nature of contraband trade. Rodríguez gained national prominence due to his participation in the military actions that first brought the Colorado Party into power in 1947 and that helped Stroessner establish his dictatorship in 1954.

Rodríguez's close relationship with Alfredo Stroessner led to his promotion as commander of the First Cavalry Division in 1961. His control of this post allowed him to operate *Taxi Aéreo Guaraní*, an air transport company, free of police supervision. According to reports by the Drug Enforcement Agency and Interpol (an international crime-fighting organization), his air-transport company became active first in smuggling cocaine and later, heroine.

When the Stroessner regime began to fall apart in 1988, Rodríguez's past did not block his own political ambitions. Support from Paraguayan civilian and military leaders, as well as from the U.S. government, helped him push Stroessner from power. Rodríguez formed his own political party and won the presidency in 1989.

Counterfeiting became another major industry in the area's cities. Initially, factories in Brazil and Paraguay made copies of designer clothes for sale to tourists who traveled to the tri-border region in search of bargains. By the 1980s, though, small shops spread through Puerto Stroessner and Foz do Iguaçú in which individuals illegally copied videotapes and computer software. The operations grew in scale and sophistication. In concert with Chinese, Korean, South Asian, and Middle Eastern operations, warehouses in the tri-border region stored counterfeit or stolen electronics for distribution across South America. The counterfeit shops also began making fake passports, visas, identity cards, and licenses. With the spread of the Internet, the tri-border region quickly developed into an active center of "identity theft" and related crimes.[67]

In its promotion of all lines of development, the Stroessner dictatorship brought dramatic changes to the tri-border region. Commercial farming expanded dramatically. Tourism and commerce boomed. The illegal but sanctioned smuggling of drugs, counterfeiting, stolen goods, and contraband became the area's economic core.

Thousands of migrants moved into the area in search of work and opportunity. Many moved to Brazil, where it was easier and cheaper to find a place to live, and traveled to work every day in Paraguay. Paraguayan border guards allowed individuals to cross into Paraguay at will. Thousands of trucks carried goods to and from Argentina and Brazil each day. Few shipments were inspected and fewer still were impounded. Little stood in the way of the legal and illegal commerce that linked Puerto Stroessner to the wider world.

By design, Alfredo Stroessner's policies undermined the security and authority of borders and boundaries. This practice resulted in an integration of peoples and activities that had not existed in the area since the start of the Independence Wars. Residents of Brazil cross the Friendship Bridge that links Foz do Iguaçú with Ciudad del Este. They work in the shops and industries located there, where goods produced legally and illegally find the freest of markets. Many support themselves by carrying goods across the borders. Argentine tourists cross from Puerto Iguazú to buy electronics, DVDs, and CDs at a fraction of what they would cost in Buenos Aires. Paraguayans spend their day crossing both borders with boxes and cartons of merchandise on their shoulders. They make their way in defiance of the borders that governments assert and patrol.

9

A Land
of Immigrants

From the beginning, the tri-border region was sparsely populated. The Guaraní settlements were larger than others in the
surrounding area, but the dispersed nature of their communities
kept the population density low. Spanish colonial policies did little to bring settlers to the region. Although Brazilian authorities
claimed control over much of the region, they did nothing to
encourage settlement through the nineteenth century.

The War of the Triple Alliance made apparent the need to
populate the land. As a result of Brazil's costly war victory, that
country gained the right to dictate the area's borders. The distance between Guairá and the Atlantic coast made the region
unattractive for both investors and settlers, however. Argentina,
concerned about border security and hoping to create new
industries and expand trade, promoted farmer colonies in the
area. Again, distance and isolation caused all but a few of these
attempts to fail.

Paraguay had perhaps the most pressing need to fill its empty
lands. The war had decimated its population. By some estimates,
more than 60 percent of those alive at the start of the conflict
died. However, once the Paraguan government got back on its
feet, it began to promote immigration. Like many countries in
the nineteenth century, Paraguay advertised in Europe for settlers. It authorized land grants and other aid programs. The
country had little luck, however. Paraguay's isolation appealed to
few who made the trip across the Atlantic.

A massive sale of public land in the 1870s did produce a
handful of private colonization schemes. One of the most
notable was Lincolnshire. British speculators, who participated
in the public land sales that took place in the 1870s, recruited
settlers among the destitute of London. Shipped to Paraguay in
1872 and 1873, the Londoners were dumped west of the Alto
Paraná River and told to farm. Lacking the tools and the skills,
the scheme ended in disaster. Scores died before the British government managed to organize their return to London in 1874. In
the 1880s, cooperative and socialist experiments launched a
handful of immigrant colonies. In every case, the lack of

resources and internal divisions undermined the experiments. News of the failed "colonization" programs damaged efforts to attract European immigrants to Paraguay for decades.[68]

In 1904, the national government enacted a less restrictive code for immigration. Only decades after it fought a disastrous war over its border claims, the government essentially dropped all serious restrictions, with two exceptions: It banned Asian immigration, and it forbade the sale of land to foreigners living within 150 miles of its borders. Paraguay's reforms effectively undermined its chances for repopulation. Within a decade, war in Europe would end the massive flow of immigrants to South America. At the same time, thousands of Asians continued to seek opportunities abroad. Restrictions that blocked them from the United States led many to South America. As this immigrant flow developed elsewhere, Paraguay decided to block people it viewed as "undesirable." It did repeal the ban in 1924, but by then, Asian immigration had declined.

Before World War II, Paraguay hosted a few successful immigrant colonies. Most notable were the Mennonites. A strict religious community, the Mennonites faced repression in some parts of central and eastern Europe and in Russia. For their needs, Paraguay's isolation was ideal. Paraguay, in turn, did its best to attract the Mennonites. Beginning in 1921, the national government passed special laws that granted them legal and economic control over any towns they formed, made settlers exempt from paying taxes and serving in the military, and guaranteed religious freedom. The government hoped that the creation of towns and farms in the Chaco would help hold off Bolivian claims to Paraguay's unpopulated western area.

Mennonite families formed settlements in the Chaco region between 1928 and 1948. More than 6,000 settlers immigrated to the Chaco. Their efforts brought a small but profitable variety of farms, dairies, and ranches to the region. The settlers received substantial aid from Mennonite communities in the United States and elsewhere. After World War II, a second generation of Mennonite immigrants built autonomous colonies in the

In 1921, the government of Paraguay passed a series of laws promoting settlement by the Mennonites, a nonconformist Protestant religious group. The government granted them legal and economic control over any towns they formed, made settlers exempt from paying taxes and serving in the military, and guaranteed religious freedom.

departments of San Pedro, just east of the Paraguay River, and Caaguazú, located west of the department of Alto Paraná.[69]

Before the Mennonites settled the area, private efforts established colonies of German immigrants on Paraguay's southeastern frontier. Hohenau, located in Itapúa, was the first of a series of settlements started in 1900. When Hohenau was founded, its isolation allowed the immigrants to set up German schools and other facilities that helped the settlers maintain a distinct lifestyle. The immigrants managed to cultivate their own yerba mate groves, which helped them gain a foothold in the yerba mate trade during and after World War I. The settlers also produced industrial crops, such as flaxseed and tung (the oil of which is used for wood preservation), for export.

In the 1920s, German settlers followed the political events of their homeland closely. Local opinion embraced Adolf Hitler, and in 1931, the settlers were active in the first branch of the Nazi Party founded in Latin America. Some of the settlers cultivated a close relationship with conservative elements in the Paraguayan army, which helped their colonies maintain their relative independence. After the war, the German colonies became one of many havens in South America for German war criminals. Josef Mengele was the most notorious of the exiles. After escaping to Argentina in 1947, Mengele was able to operate freely in Buenos Aires's business community for years. However, international agencies stepped up their efforts to bring war criminals to justice by the end of the 1950s. Fearing possible capture, he fled to Paraguay in 1959 and hid among the sympathetic German colonists for a year before he moved to Brazil.

Other small European colonies, sponsored by private companies, appeared in the tri-border region. In 1927, a multinational group founded the settlement of Fram, also located in Itapúa. Austrian and Czechoslovakian immigrants built towns in Guairá, where they developed Paraguay's commercial wine industry.

The Stroessner dictatorship promoted immigration much more effectively. Simple laws and few restrictions made Paraguay relatively attractive for travelers and settlers from all parts of the world. Since the regime directed immigrants away from Asunción and the central region of the country, most of the new arrivals settled in the departments of the tri-border region.

The Japanese were the first large contingent of Asian immigrants to settle in Paraguay. Although the first small Japanese immigrant colony appeared outside the tri-border region in 1936, large-scale immigration from Japan came as a result of a plan backed by the Paraguayan and Japanese governments and launched in 1959. The Japanese settled in three colonies: Colonia

Yguazú was established just north of Ciudad del Este; Colonia Fram and Colonia Alto Paraná were both located in Itapúa. The colonies were established to grow grains and raise cattle for both the local and the Japanese markets. Japan, with its large population crowded onto its home islands, lacked sufficient land for farming. As a result, the demand for the settlement's harvests grew, and the colonies expanded. They maintained themselves as cultural islands, separated by language, cultural habits, and social practices from the country that surrounded them, but their agricultural production helped develop Paraguay's farming sector and increase the country's exports. Like the earlier successful colonies, the Japanese settlements received aid from the home country. The Japanese government, which regarded the colonies as almost an extension of their territory in economic terms, provided financial support and technical assistance as the colonies developed their agricultural industries. By 1990, more than 85,000 Japanese had settled in Paraguay.[70]

Unlike the Japanese, Korean immigration relied on private resources and established regulations. Officially, 9,000 Koreans immigrated to the tri-border region between 1965 and 1990. This grossly understates the true number of Koreans who have settled in the country. Korean immigrants settled almost exclusively in Ciudad del Este. They became a key part of the international trade, both legal and illegal, that developed in Ciudad del Este since its creation as a tax-free trading and tourist zone. Korean immigrants helped develop the workshops and factories that fueled the city's rapid growth since the 1970s. They still play a leading role in the retail sector of the city's central commercial district.[71]

Immigrants from China initially followed the pattern of the Korean settlers. At first, the Paraguayan government helped coordinate the initial wave of Chinese immigrants in the late 1970s. Then, as their numbers increased, Chinese immigration passed beyond the control of Paraguayan officials. Some estimate that as many as 50,000 East Asian immigrants, mostly Chinese and Koreans—a fifth of the city's population—live and work in Ciudad del Este. This large Chinese community has been plagued by Chinese and Taiwanese criminal gangs that extended their operations into the tri-border region in the 1980s. These gangs extort cash and promote the sale of stolen and counterfeit goods in the city's shops. They also use the city as a base for transporting drugs from Asia to American and European markets.[72]

As immigration from East Asia grew dramatically, the tri-border region also experienced a sharp rise in the number of Muslim immigrants. When Israel invaded Lebanon in 1982, a large number of Lebanese and Palestinian people immigrated to the Americas. The lack of travel restrictions led as many as 30,000 Muslim immigrants to settle in the tri-border region. Though they may work in Ciudad del Este, competing with Asian immigrants and Paraguayan nationals for a share of legal and contraband trade, most Muslim settlers live across the border in Foz do Iguaçú.[73]

The Korean, Chinese, and Muslim immigrant communities in the tri-border region internationalized the area. They continue to rely on their traditional languages, they maintain their cultural lives in the fashion of their home countries, and they rely on international contacts and partners in their daily business. The immigrants have helped transform Ciudad del Este. Economists rank it as one of the world's most vibrant commercial centers.[74]

For Paraguay, Asian immigration has had a profound effect on the tri-border region but little impact on the rest of the country. The Stroessner regime promoted Asian immigration as part of a broad plan to create industry and encourage economic development. It made no effort to assimilate the immigrants. Consequently, significant areas of the region now seem to belong in a different continent. Ciudad del Este became a multinational urban center. Visitors conduct business in a variety of languages and pay for goods and services with Asian, American, and European currencies.

The most significant immigrant community to arrive in

The Friendship Bridge, which opened in 1965, spans the Upper Paraná River and connects Foz do Iguaçú, Brazil, with Ciudad del Este, Paraguay. Approximately 30,000 to 40,000 people cross the bridge daily to work in one of the two cities.

Paraguay since 1960—the Brazilians—had the simplest course to travel. Paraguayan law placed restrictions on Brazilian travel and immigration in the wake of the War of the Triple Alliance. Until the 1960s, it maintained a ban on foreign ownership of land in the eastern border area that made it impossible for Brazilians to live in the Paraguayan parts of the tri-border region. This ban had not been an issue in previous generations because of the general lack of interest within Brazil in the western lands of Paraná state. In the nineteenth century, however, the government created a security corridor that blocked the sale and settlement of public lands along its border with Paraguay. Through the 1950s, the forests mattered more than the land: Instead of settlement, private companies bought or rented land in the tri-border region and developed a regional lumber industry there.[75]

In the 1960s, population growth and the extension of roads and rail lines into the area made the land much more valuable. A rush of squatters and speculators moved to take control of the land. They quickly cleared the remaining forests that for centuries had limited overland travel between Brazil and Paraguay. Within a few years, the demand for land exceeded the supply. When the Friendship Bridge opened in 1965, the highway connecting Paraguay and Brazil made it easy for workers to live on one side of the border and work on the other. Brazilians were the first to take advantage of the new opportunity. In recent years, 30,000 to 40,000 people cross the bridge each day to visit or work in Ciudad del Este or Foz do Iguaçú.[76]

Beyond the cities, the eastern departments of Paraguay attracted thousands of settlers after 1967, when the Paraguayan government repealed its agrarian statute, which banned foreign land ownership. Brazilian immigrants poured into the area and pushed out the remaining Amerindian communities that had survived in isolation for centuries. Within five years, at least 30,000 Brazilians had taken up land for farming in eastern Paraguay. The construction of Itaipú Dam and the explosive growth of Ciudad del Este's commercial economy attracted thousands more. Although hundreds of thousands of Paraguayans moved into the area in response to the same opportunities that attracted migrants and immigrants, the foreign communities have emerged as the leading force in the economic growth of both the urban and the rural sectors of the regional economy.[77]

When the commercial potential of the tri-border region grew in the 1960s, the area attracted waves of migrants and immigrants that were unprecedented in size and diversity. Although the rapid pace of growth east of the Alto Paraná River turned a wilderness into a crowded land, the changes that took place to the west were more striking and significant. The settlers populated this empty corner of Paraguay. They provided the human capital that helped the Stroessner dictatorship realize its dream of economic growth.

Whereas the immigrants changed the tri-border region, the nations nominally in charge of the area had little impact on the new settlers. As was the case with the European colonies decades before, the immigrants formed distinct communities and worked to maintain their lifestyles in a foreign land. In Paraguay, especially, the new arrivals changed the tri-border region into a unique world.

10

Adjusting to
New Challenges

After September 11, 2001, life in the tri-border region changed dramatically. Led by the United States, government officials around the globe committed their countries to the fight against the threat of international terrorism. They identified the tri-border region as a key training and fund-raising center—one that supported the most dangerous terrorist organizations. They announced their governments' commitment to isolating and dismantling the foundations of the international structures that supported this grave threat.

The residents of Ciudad del Este noticed changes immediately. Paraguayan security forces conducted raids of exchange houses and commercial shops only three days after the attacks in New York and Washington, D.C. They seized financial records, counterfeit goods, forged documents, and cash. They also detained dozens of individuals who the authorities later identified as being linked with terrorist organizations.[78]

Months later, security became tighter on the Brazilian side of the frontier. Border patrols seized trucks with illegal cargoes; raided jungle airstrips that once allowed smugglers to transport drugs, weapons, and other contraband into Brazil; and arrested suspected ringleaders in a series of raids in and around Foz do Iguaçú. Residents of the border region expressed both shock and disappointment. Paraguayan merchants asserted that their shops and stores deliver bargains, not funds for terrorists.

The changes continued. News reports broadcasted the realities of the area. The public and casual nature of smuggling suggested that criminal behavior was acceptable and even tolerated by the border police. Police records also revealed a shocking level of violent crime. Rates for assault and murder in Puerto Iguazú, Foz do Iguaçú, and Ciudad del Este climbed to the highest levels recorded in Argentina, Brazil, and Paraguay, respectively. Assaults and murders of business owners, who are the targets of organized crime, became a constant threat. Robberies of tourists, in the cities and even on the Friendship Bridge between Foz do Iguaçú and Ciudad del Este, rose.[79]

The region's link to terrorism quickly depressed the tourist

The 1991 Treaty of Asunción established the Mercosur agreement, which promotes free trade between the countries of Argentina, Brazil, Paraguay, and Uruguay. Thanks to uniform tariffs and taxes, the agreement has reduced some of the small-scale smuggling in the tri-border region, but the movement of such items as automobiles and illegal weapons continues to be a problem. Pictured here are representatives at the nineteenth-annual Mercosur summit in 2000.

industry. With fewer visitors, the tourist industry went into recession. In addition, increased border security, adopted in part to convince foreign visitors that the Iguazú area was safe, interfered with large- and small-scale smuggling. With increased security affecting both tourism and smuggling, the tri-border region appeared to be in crisis.

The area's economic slump is not simply a product of the terrorist activity. The Mercosur agreement, first proposed as a trade pact involving Argentina and Brazil in 1991 and then launched in full force in 1995, set in motion a series of changes that have made it harder for the tri-border region to operate as a commercial-, political-, and judicial-free zone. MERCOSUR is an acronym for the "Mercado Común del Sur" (in English, "Common Market of the South"); it came into being as a result of an agreement reached among the countries of Argentina,

Brazil, Paraguay, and Uruguay. By signing the treaty, which laid out points of economic integration and an ideal schedule for increased integration, the four countries' leaders backed a vehicle that promised economic growth and prosperity through increased intraregional trade.

Before the implementation of Mercosur's proposed reforms in the 1990s, currency values, tax rates, labor regulations, and tariffs separated the neighboring countries' economies. Mercosur represented a movement away from the arbitrary assertion of borders and divisions that in the past had put port

ASSAD AHMAD BARAKAT: HEZBOLLAH'S "RINGLEADER" IN FOZ DO IGUAÇÚ

After the 1992 bombing of the Israeli Embassy in Buenos Aires and the September 11, 2001, attacks in New York and Washington, D.C., concerns over the presence of terrorist cells in the Americas have grown immeasurably. The tri-border region, with its diverse and sizeable immigrant population, and due to its connection with contraband trade and other illegal activities, became the focus of investigation by international authorities.

Security agencies in the United States, Paraguay, and Argentina found evidence of terrorist activity in Ciudad del Este, Foz do Iguaçú, and the countryside surrounding the two largest cities in the tri-border region. Rumors spread. After news appeared of the discovery of tourist posters and brochures about Iguazú Falls in the possession of Taliban and al Qaeda soldiers in Afghanistan in 2002, Brazilian journalists reported that Osama bin Laden and other al Qaeda leaders visited a mosque in Foz do Iguaçú.

The accuracy of such reports remains difficult to determine. Military and police forces in the region have instead focused on confirmed activists as part of a broad effort to strengthen security measures in the tri-border region.

One key target in recent years has been Assad Ahmad Barakat, who fled Lebanon as a teenager with his father during a violent phase in the war there. In 1985, he arrived in Paraguay and began to work in the city's business community. He succeeded and settled in Foz do Iguaçú, which has the area's largest Muslim community (estimated at 20,000 to 30,000). The Brazilian cities into competition with one another and led countries to war. Saddled with debt and economic stagnation, the leaders of the partner countries agreed to pull down the economic boundaries that had separated their countries. They hoped that the unification of four economic islands would lead to economic growth broad enough and deep enough to benefit all concerned.

The Mercosur agreement launched reforms that gradually lessened the tariffs placed on imports from other member nations. Beginning in 1995, it created a customs union that gave producers and consumers matched conditions. In theory, the

border city's mosques and community centers also make it more attractive for Lebanese and other Muslim immigrants.

According to Argentine, Paraguayan, and U.S. agents who monitor the immigrant communities in the region, Barakat became the key backer of Hezbollah in the area; through his companies, he funneled millions of dollars to support the group. He also was active in money-laundering and smuggling operations that connected Paraguay and Brazil with Hezbollah and its operations in Lebanon and Palestine.

On September 14, 2001, Paraguayan police raided a number of businesses in Ciudad del Este. According to press reports, they discovered evidence that connected Barakat and his companies with terrorist activities around the globe. Soon, Argentine authorities issued a warrant for his arrest in connection with the bombings of the Israeli Embassy (1992) and the Argentine-Israeli Mutual Aid Association (AIMA) Community Center (1994) in Buenos Aires.

Barakat remained free in Brazil until 2003. Under pressure from its neighbors and the United States, the Brazilian government arrested and extradited Barakat to Paraguay. He was convicted of tax evasion and sentenced to six and a half years in prison.

Although Paraguayan officials advertise Barakat's detention as a sign of their greater commitment to the fight against terrorism, his neighbors remain adamant that the "donations" that Barakat and others sent voluntarily to Hezbollah support humanitarian programs vital for the recovery of Lebanon and Palestine.

reforms and the opening of the customs union would have allowed producers in any of the countries the opportunity to produce and market their products—grains, sugar, automobiles, or shoes—to consumers in four countries instead of one. In practice, what was agreed to and what was done were two different things.

Initially, the opening of the Brazilian market to imports from neighboring countries benefited Argentina the most. The large Brazilian market allowed Argentine farmers, ranchers, and manufacturers to increase output and sales dramatically. As it became clear that, for a variety of reasons, the other member countries of Mercosur were not benefiting as much, governments imposed inspection requirements, transport regulations, or customs procedures that slowed this freer flow of trade across borders.

In 1999, the first serious challenge threatened the Mercosur pact. The Brazilian government, in reaction to a variety of economic problems, devalued its country's currency. Policy makers hoped that this move would promote Brazilian exports to Europe and North America. However, the devaluation instantly made Argentine imports uncompetitive in the Brazilian market. Given a competitive advantage, Brazilian farmers and manufacturers replaced Argentine suppliers and Argentina's economy spun into recession.

As it turned out, Mercosur's problems gave those who worked in the illegal trades of the tri-border region renewed hope. The slow implementation of the trade pact, the maintenance of many trade regulations, and disputes over currency values created space for smuggling, counterfeiting, and other activities that had fueled economic growth in the area before 1995. At a critical point, negotiations between Argentina and Brazil rescued the agreement. The negotiated settlement adjusted currency values and effectively reopened the Brazilian market for Argentine products after 2001. The settlement also made the relationship between the pact's two most important members stronger in the end.[80]

This positive step for South America's two largest countries was a disaster for the merchants and workers of the tri-border region, however. In 1995, Ciudad del Este's commercial zone generated trade worth $4.2 billion. Illegal transactions, ranging from cigarette smuggling to the sale of weapons, stolen goods, and drugs, generated billions more. In 2000, the value of legal sales fell to less than $1.5 billion.[81] The Paraguayan government announced plans to follow the model that Argentina presented. It hoped to attract foreign capital and build reassembly plants, or *maquiladoras*, that would take component parts and assemble manufactured goods, like automobiles or appliances, for the Brazilian and Argentine markets. Political instability in Argentina, Brazil, and Paraguay, and the slowed expansion of the Mercosur economies since 2001 have blocked such progress. Government officials then suggested that tourism might replace some of the profits and jobs lost in the commercial sector if the public and private sector invested in roads, hotels, and transit facilities.

The terrorist threat has helped stall this initiative, as well. Puerto Iguazú is now much more tightly patrolled. Fewer foreign tourists and fewer nationals from other parts of Argentina or Brazil travel to the border region for shopping or vacation.[82] It has also brought new international forces into the tri-border region. Argentina was the first to agree to joint training exercises with the U.S. military in the wake of the September 11 attacks. For the U.S. government, the alleged connections between the tri-border region and terrorist groups, combined with the region's history of counterfeiting and smuggling operations, made it a significant threat to hemispheric security.

In 2004, Paraguay also agreed to participate in joint military exercises with U.S. military forces. The U.S. government provided $2.5 million for training and equipping the region's security forces to meet the challenge of international terrorist operations. Although Brazil has not agreed to coordinate its activities with those of the United States, its government announced plans to modernize its security infrastructure and

THE MANY FACES OF CONTRABAND TRADE

The economies of the tri-border region cities, especially Foz do Iguaçú and Ciudad del Este, are based on contraband trade. Alfredo Stroessner and his government promoted this practice when Ciudad del Este came into being; Foz do Iguaçú's illegal trade developed in response to the growth of tourism and trade since the 1960s. Traditionally, locals identified contraband as belonging to one of two categories: that of the "ant" and that of the "elephant." Elephant contraband was large in scale and organized by local and international traders. Stolen automobiles, illegal weapons, large shipments of electronics, manufactured goods, and other items moved through Paraguay via a transitory market system. For example, automobiles stolen in Buenos Aires would receive new counterfeit license plates and registration papers that helped speed their sale in urban Brazil. Or, manufactured goods produced in Brazil would move on trucks through Paraguay and into Argentina, where agents sold them to customers, free of taxes and other duties.

For the poor living in the tri-border region, *contrabando hormiga*—"ant contraband"—helped them survive from day to day. Playing a game against the tax collectors in Argentina or Brazil, thousands of people hired by merchants in Paraguay would carry goods from the country, where prices and taxes were relatively low, across the bridges that connected the area's neighboring cities and undersell the same items in the neighboring city, where prices and taxes were high. Cigarettes, clothing, even cooking oil became staples of this illegal but tolerated trading system. After collecting a few cents for each package, many would pick up another shipment for the return trip. A day's effort provided the only employment for many until 1995.

The launching of Mercosur (the Southern Common Market) reduced the opportunities for "ant" smugglers, because tariff and tax rates became more uniform. Although the smuggling of everyday items continues, Paraguayan merchants now put more weight behind a relatively new line of smugglers: the *sacoleiros*. Often called informal importers, these "bag carriers" buy large quantities of counterfeit clothes, electronics, DVDs, or computer games in Ciudad del Este. They then transport their wares to Brazil's cities, where they become merchants in "Paraguayan" markets. In 2005, efforts by the Brazilian government to stop such trade led to police blockades of border roads and mass protests on the Friendship Bridge that connects Foz do Iguaçú and Ciudad del Este.

Although the Mercosur agreement has made it more difficult for smugglers to move contraband from Paraguay to Brazil, they have turned to using bags to transport large quantities of counterfeit clothes, electronics, DVDs, or computer games from Ciudad del Este into Brazil. Pictured here are smugglers crossing the border from Paraguay into Brazil.

increase its training of military and police forces in charge of protecting its border with Paraguay.[83]

Frustration over current circumstances has led residents of the tri-border region to protest. Civic leaders ask for specific evidence of terrorist links and activities. Evidence of financial support for Hezbollah and other Middle Eastern organizations is ample and clear, but although the U.S. government defined this as offering support for terrorism, the individuals and the groups that send donations disagreed. They regard Hezbollah, Hamas, and the community organizations in Lebanon and Palestine that they support as legal and legitimate groups that serve their home communities.

A few believe that something sinister lies behind the terrorism accusations. Progressive groups organized a regional "Social Forum" in June 2004. In presentations for the public and the international press, the forum presenters offered reminders of the difficulties that the poor and the working class faced as a result of the economic shifts and policy changes that Mercosur and the antiterrorist push brought about. Some claimed that the terrorist threat was manufactured—that it hid an attempt by international corporations to take control of the water and other natural resources in the tri-border region.[84]

With unemployment rising and the traditional avenues for employment restricted, the tri-border region's boom may be at an end. Some residents have already moved on: Drug traffickers have carved out new landing strips in the more isolated northern departments of Paraguay; counterfeiters have shifted their operations to other free-trade zones in South America; and migrants have moved to other cities where opportunities are more abundant. Despite the challenges, people and goods still cross the borders. The increased security that recent events have brought to the region slow the movement of people and goods, but even the most aggressive show of force presents only a temporary clamp on the human and material relationships that unite the region.

1492 Christopher Columbus successfully leads the first Iberian expedition to the Americas.

1494 The Treaty of Tordesillas establishes a line separating Spanish- and Portuguese-controlled territories in the Western Hemisphere.

1516 An expedition led by Spanish explorer Juan Díaz de Solís makes landfall in the Río de la Plata estuary.

1524 Portuguese sailor Alejo García leads an expedition across Brazil into Paraguay.

1526 Sebastian Cabot leads an expedition up the Paraguay River.

1536 Pedro de Mendoza founds the first settlement of Buenos Aires.

1537 An expedition from Buenos Aires establishes the settlement of Asunción.

1544 Paraguayan rebels force Governor Álvar Núñez Cabeza de Vaca from power in Asunción.

1587 The first Jesuit missionaries arrive in Paraguay.

1610 Jesuits build the first missions in the tri-border region.

1628 Bandeirantes begin their attacks of missions and settlements in the tri-border region.

1641 Jesuits relocate their missions to the Alto Paraná River basin.

1720 The Comunero Revolt begins.

1735 Combined Spanish and Guaraní militia forces defeat the last of the Comunero rebels.

1750 Treaty of Madrid grants land south of the Alto Paraná River, where the Jesuits had established their missions, to Portugal as part of a settlement of the boundaries that separated Spanish and Portuguese South America.

1754 Guaraní War begins.

1761 Treaty of San Ildefonso returns mission territories to Spain.

1767 Jesuits are expelled from Spanish America.

1776 Spain creates the Viceroyalty of the Río de la Plata, with Buenos Aires as its capital.

1806 Militia in Buenos Aires defeats a British invading force.

1807 Spanish militia, reinforced by a large force of Guaraní soldiers, defeats a second British attack, in the Río de la Plata estuary.

1808 Spanish Crown toppled by Napoleon.

1810 Town councils in Buenos Aires and Asunción assume colonial authority; Buenos Aires declares its independence.

1811 Town council in Asunción declares independence.

1814 José Gaspar Rodríguez de Francia begins his reign as the leader of Paraguay.

1820 José Gervasio Artigas goes into exile in Paraguay.

1825 Federalist forces defeat the unitarios and thwart

1494
The Treaty of Tordesillas establishes a line separating Spanish- and Portuguese-controlled territories in the Western Hemisphere

1610
Jesuits build the first missions in the tri-border region

1767
Jesuits are expelled from Spanish America

1494   1776

1537
An expedition from Buenos Aires establishes the settlement of Asunción

1754
Guaraní War begins

1776
Spain creates the Viceroyalty of the Río de la Plata

attempts to reunite the regions of the old viceroyalty into one country.

1829 Juan Manuel de Rosas becomes governor of Buenos Aires Province.

1840 José Gaspar Rodríguez De Francia dies.

1844 Carlos Antonio López gains power in Paraguay.

1862 After his father's death, Francisco Solano López becomes dictator of Paraguay.

1864 Paraguay's invasion of Corrientes sets in motion the War of the Triple Alliance.

1870 Brazilian offensive ends the War of the Triple Alliance; Francisco Solano López is killed at the Battle of Cerro Cora; Brazilian and Argentine armies occupy Paraguay for five years.

1814
José Gaspar Rodríguez de Francia begins his reign as leader of Paraguay

1954
Alfredo Stroessner seizes control of the presidency in Paraguay

1973
Itaipú Treaty between Brazil and Paraguay leads to construction of Itaipú Dam

1814   **1995**

1870
Brazilian offensive ends the War of the Triple Alliance

1965
The Friendship Bridge opens

1995
Mercosur agreement goes into effect

1881 Argentine Confederation creates Misiones Territory.

1886 La Industria Paraguay forms—it becomes Paraguay's largest landowner and leads the revival of the yerba mate industry in the tri-border region.

1900 Hohenau, a colony of German immigrants, is established.

1932 Chaco War between Paraguay and Bolivia begins.

1947 Colorado Party returns to power in Paraguay.

1954 Alfredo Stroessner seizes control of the presidency in Paraguay.

1957 Puerto Stroessner founded; renamed Ciudad del Este in 1989.

1965 The Friendship Bridge that connects Puerto Stroessner and the Brazilian city of Foz do Iguaçú opens.

1966 Act of Ygauzú gives Brazil authority over Guairá Falls; Paraguay and Brazil agree to jointly develop the hydroelectric potential of the Alto Paraná.

1967 Repeal of Paraguay's Agrarian Statute allows Brazilians to purchase land in border areas.

1973 Itaipú Treaty establishes partnership between Brazil and Paraguay that leads to the construction of the Itaipú Dam.

1989 Alfredo Stroessner is forced from power by a military coup; General Andrés Rodriguez Pedotti assumes the presidency.

1992 Israeli Embassy in Buenos Aires is bombed; investigations link Muslim groups in the tri-border region with the crime.

1994 Argentine-Israeli Mutual Aid Association (AIMA) Cultural Center in Buenos Aires is bombed; suspicions of foreign links to the crime lead Argentina to tighten border security near Puerto Iguazú.

1995 Agreement that launches the Mercosur common market among Argentina, Brazil, Paraguay, and Uruguay goes into effect.

2004 Argentine military engages in joint exercises with forces from the United States in the tri-border region.

Chapter 1

1. For a list of news reports relating to the attacks, visit the Wikipedia Web page on the AIMA bombing: *http://en.wikipedia.org/wiki/AIMA_bombing*.
2. For details, see Jeffrey Goldberg, "In the Party of God," *The New Yorker* (October 28, 2002).
3. The U.S. State Department has posted Taylor's remarks on its Web site. See *http://www.state.gov/s/ct/rls/rm/2001/5674.htm*.
4. A review of these reports (denied by spokespeople for the Muslim communities in the tri-border region) appears in Library of Congress, *Terrorist and Organized Crime Groups in the Tri-border Area (TBA) of South America: A Report Prepared by the Federal Research Division, Library of Congress, Under an Interagency Agreement with the United States Government*. Washington, DC: Federal Research Division, Library of Congress, 2003, pp. 14–24.
5. Ibid., pp. 9–10.
6. Sebastian Rotella describes the role that Middle Eastern immigrants played in the tri-border region's legal and illegal trade in "Jungle Hub for World's Outlaws," *Los Angeles Times* (August 24, 1998).
7. An appendix listing the operatives and groups that security officials link with the region appears in Library of Congress, *Terrorist and Organized Crime Groups*, pp. 71–80.
8. Ibid., pp. 20–24.
9. Ibid., pp. 4–11.

Chapter 2

10. Thomas Whigham provides a good description of the river systems and their rhythms in *The Politics of River Trade: Tradition and Development in the Upper Plata, 1780–1870*. Albuquerque: University of New Mexico Press, 1991, pp. 4–7.
11. Guillermo Tell Bertoni and J. Richard Gorham, "The Geography of Paraguay," in J. Richard Gorham, ed., *Paraguay: Ecological Essays*. Miami, FL: Academy of the Arts and Sciences of the Americas, 1973, pp. 10–12.
12. Guillermo T. Bertoni and J. Richard Gorham, "The People of Paraguay: Origin and Numbers," in J. Richard Gorham, *Paraguay: Ecological Essays*, pp. 124–125.
13. Elman Service, *Spanish-Guarani Relations in Early Colonial Paraguay*. Westport, CT: Greenwood Press, 1971, pp. 15–18.
14. Ibid.
15. Ibid., p. 18.

Chapter 3

16. For a narrative of the exploration and settlement phase and citations of more detailed works, see David Rock, *Argentina, 1516–1982*. Berkeley: University of California Press, 1985, pp. 6–14.
17. For a discussion of the different ways in which the Iberians explored the Americas and built their empires, see John Chasteen, *Born in Blood and Fire: A Concise History of Latin America*. New York: W. W. Norton, 2001, pp. 29–48.
18. For details on the interaction between the Spanish and the Guaraní, see Service, *Spanish-Guaraní Relations*, pp. 18–23.
19. For a more detailed review of this period, see Adalberto López, *The Revolt of the Comuñeros, 1721–1735: A Study in the Colonial History of Paraguay*. Cambridge, MA: Schenkman, 1976, pp. 2–32.

Chapter 4

20. López, *The Revolt of the Comuñeros*, pp. 28–29.
21. For a brief overview of the Jesuits and their missions, see López, *The Revolt of the Comuñeros*, pp. 3–46.
22. Ibid., p. 36.
23. Ibid., p. 42.
24. Ibid., pp. 62–63.
25. For information on Spain's imperial history, see J. H. Elliott, "Unity and Empire, 1500–1800: Spain and Europe," in J. H. Elliot, ed., *The Spanish World: Civilization and Empire in Europe and the Americas Past and Present*. New York: Harry N. Abrams, 1991, pp. 41–56.
26. Rock, *Argentina*, pp. 52–54.

Chapter 5

27. For a detailed explanation of commercial and political relations in and around the tri-border region, see Thomas Whigham,

The Politics of River Trade: Tradition and Development in the Upper Plata, 1780–1870. Albuquerque: University of New Mexico Press, 1991, pp. 3–20.

28. For a brief overview of the shifts that Bourbon authorities imposed, see Daniel Lewis, *The History of Argentina.* New York: Palgrave, 2003, pp. 30–33.

29. John Hoyt Williams reviews conditions in the neglected northern territories of the Viceroyalty of the Río de la Plata in *The Rise and Fall of the Paraguayan Republic, 1800–1870.* Austin: University of Texas Press, 1979, pp. 10–17.

30. John Lynch provides a clear and detailed overview of the impact of European events on Spain's colonies in *The Spanish American Revolutions 1808–1826,* 2nd ed. New York: W. W. Norton, 1986, pp. 7–52.

31. Concerning the battles and their impact, see Rock, *Argentina,* pp. 71–73.

32. For a detailed description of Paraguay's resistance against Buenos Aires and ensuing developments, see Lynch, *Spanish American Revolutions,* pp. 105–118.

33. Concerning the final years of Artigas's revolt, see Whigham, *Politics of River Trade,* pp. 30–33.

Chapter 6

34. Thomas Whigham provides a recent review of the Francia dictatorship and its accomplishments in *The Paraguayan War: Causes and Early Conduct,* Vol. 1. Lincoln: University of Nebraska Press, 2002, pp. 36–41.

35. For a detailed review of Francia's military, diplomatic, and economic policies, see John Hoyt Williams, *The Rise and Fall of the Paraguayan Republic, 1800–1870.* Austin: University of Texas Press, 1979, pp. 63–74.

36. Williams, *The Rise and Fall of the Paraguayan Republic,* pp. 102–111.

37. Ibid., pp. 122–124.

38. For details concerning Rosas's dictatorship, see John Lynch, *Argentina Dictator: Juan Manuel de Rosas.* Wilmington, DE: Scholarly Resources, Inc., 2001.

39. Williams, *The Rise and Fall of the Paraguayan Republic,* pp. 140–150.

40. Ibid., pp. 150–155.

41. Ibid., pp. 177–189.

42. Whigham, *Politics of River Trade,* pp. 79–84.

43. Williams, *The Rise and Fall of the Paraguayan Republic,* pp. 195–227; and Whigham, *The Paraguayan War: Causes and Early Conduct,* Vol. 1, pp. 250–254.

Chapter 7

44. For an overview of Paraguay's political and economic trends, see Paul Lewis, "Paraguay From the War of the Triple Alliance to the Chaco War, 1870–1932," in Leslie Bethell, ed., *The Cambridge History of Latin America,* Vol. 5. New York: Cambridge University Press, 1986, pp. 475–496.

45. Robert Eidt, *Pioneer Settlement in Northeast Argentina.* Madison: University of Wisconsin Press, 1971, pp. 62–63.

46. Ibid., pp. 68–69.

47. Concerning the general effort to fill Argentina's empty spaces with settlers, see Mark Jefferson, *Peopling the Argentine People.* New York: American Geographical Society, 1926; and Daniel Lewis, *The History of Argentina.* New York: Palgrave, 2003, pp. 63–66.

48. Eidt, *Pioneer Settlement in Northeast Argentina,* pp. 71–73.

49. Ibid., pp. 80–82.

50. Ibid., pp. 186–190.

51. Joe Foweraker, *The Struggle for Land: A Political Economy of the Frontier in Brazil From 1930 to the Present Day.* Cambridge, UK: Cambridge University Press, 1981, pp. 28–34.

52. Ibid., pp. 83–84.

53. Lewis, "Paraguay," p. 480.

54. Ibid., pp. 480–481.

55. Ibid., pp. 481.

56. Ibid., pp. 483.

57. Ibid., pp. 483–484.

58. Ibid., pp. 488–490.

59. Ibid., pp. 494–495.

60. Eidt, *Pioneer Settlement,* pp. 142–146.

Chapter 8

61. Paul Lewis provides a clear narrative of the Colorado Party's rise and Stroessner's dictatorship in "Paraguay Since 1930," in Leslie Bethell, ed., *The Cambridge History of Latin America,* Vol. 8. New York: Cambridge University Press, 1991, pp. 245–265.

62. For a brief overview of the endemic nature of smuggling, see "Free Trade with

Brazil and Argentina Poses Threat to Smugglers in Ciudad del Este," *The Economist* (September 1, 1990): p. 62.

63. For details, see Werner Baer and Luis Breuer, "From Inward- to Outward-oriented Growth: Paraguay in the 1980s," *Journal of Interamerican Studies and World Affairs* 28 (Autumn 1986), 3: pp. 125–140.

64. For a detailed history of drug smuggling in Paraguay, see José Luis Simón, "Drug Addiction and Drug Trafficking in Paraguay: An Approach to the Problem During the Transition," *Journal of Interamerican Studies and World Affairs* 34 (Autumn 1992), 3: pp. 157–160.

65. Ibid.

66. For additional details, see Library of Congress, *Terrorist and Organized Crime Groups in the Tri-border Area (TBA) of South America*. Washington, DC: Federal Research Division, Library of Congress, 2003, pp. 37–60.

67. Ibid, pp. 58–60.

Chapter 9

68. R. Andrew Nickson provides brief overviews of every colonization project and most immigrant communities in his *Historical Dictionary of Paraguay*, 2nd ed. Metuchen, NJ: Scarecrow Press, 1993. Concerning the Lincolnshire scam, see pp. 348–349.

69. For information about the Mennonites' colonies, see Joseph Winfield Fretz, *Pilgrims in Paraguay*. Scottdale, PA: Herald Press, 1953.

70. The Japanese American National Museum in Los Angeles has sponsored the International Nikkei Research Project. The project Web site provides a narrative of the Japanese presence in Paraguay: *http://www.janm.org/projects/inrp/english/time_paraguay.htm*.

71. An online version of the U.S. Government Area Studies Handbook for Paraguay discusses the contours of Korean immigration. See *http://www.country-studies.com/paraguay/minority-groups.html*.

72. Library of Congress, *Transnational Activities of Chinese Crime Organizations*. Washington, DC: Federal Research Division, Library of Congress, 2003, pp. 21–22.

73. Library of Congress, *Terrorist and Organized Crime Groups in the Tri-border Area (TBA) of South America*. Washington, DC: Federal Research Division, Library of Congress, 2003, pp. 9–10.

74. Ibid, pp. 10–11.

75. For an overview of the exploitation and eventual settlement of Brazil's southwestern territories, see Joe Foweraker, *The Struggle for Land: A Political Economy of the Pioneer Frontier in Brazil From 1930 to the Present Day*. Cambridge, UK: Cambridge University Press, 1981, pp. 83–105.

76. Library of Congress, *Terrorist and Organized Crime Groups in the Tri-border Area*, p. 11.

77. Alejandro Sciscioli, "Tension Over Presence of 'Brasiguayos.'" Interpress Service News Agency for Tierramérica Network, November 21, 2003.

Chapter 10

78. Goldberg, "In the Party of God."

79. Major newspapers in the United States and Europe filed regular reports about changing conditions in the region after September 11. See, for example, Hector Tobar and Paula Gobbi, "Response to Terror," *The Los Angeles Times* (December 26, 2001).

80. See Laura Gómez Mera, "Explaining Mercosur's Survival: Strategic Sources of Argentine–Brazilian Convergence," *Journal of Latin American Studies* 37 (February 2005), 1: pp. 109–141.

81. Marcel Ballve, "A Small Nation Looks for Its Role in the Global Script: The Americas Move Toward a Single Free-Trade Zone by 2005, Paraguay Asks if It Will Share the Bounty," *Christian Science Monitor* (April 24, 2001): p. 7.

82. Peter Hudson, "'There are no Terrorists Here'; In a Lawless No Man's Land Deep in the Heart of South America, Muslims Face Down a Suspicious World," *Newsweek International*, Atlantic Edition (November 19, 2001): p. 39.

83. Randall Wood, "Of Note: South America's Tri-border Region," *SAIS Review*.

84. Marcela Valente, "South America: A Giant Aquifer and Rumors of Terrorists," *Inter Press Service* (February 18, 2004). *http://www.factiva.com* (October 14, 2004).

Baer, Werner, and Luis Breuer. "From Inward- to Outward-Oriented Growth: Paraguay in the 1980s." *Journal of Interamerican Studies and World Affairs* 28 (Autumn 1986), 3: 125–140.

Ballve, Marcel. "A Small Nation Looks for Its Role in the Global Script: The Americas Move Toward a Single Free-Trade Zone by 2005, Paraguay Asks if It Will Share the Bounty." *Christian Science Monitor* (April 24, 2001): 7.

Bethell, Leslie, ed. *The Cambridge History of Latin America.* 11 vols. New York: Cambridge University Press, 1984–1991.

Chasteen, John. *Born in Blood and Fire: A Concise History of Latin America.* New York: W. W. Norton, 2001.

Eidt, Robert. *Pioneer Settlement in Northeast Argentina.* Madison: University of Wisconsin Press, 1971.

Elliot, J. H., ed. *The Spanish World: Civilization and Empire in Europe and the Americas Past and Present.* New York: Harry N. Abrams, 1991.

Foweraker, Joe. *The Struggle for Land: A Political Economy of the Pioneer Frontier in Brazil from 1930 to the Present Day.* Cambridge: Cambridge University Press, 1981.

Fretz, Joseph Winfield. *Pilgrims in Paraguay: The Story of Mennonite Colonization in South America.* Scottdale, PA: Herald Press, 1953.

Gómez Mera, Laura. "Explaining MERCOSUR's Survival: Strategic Sources of Argentine-Brazilian Convergence." *Journal of Latin American Studies* 37 (February 2005), 1: 109–141.

Gorham, J. Richard, ed. *Paraguay: Ecological Essays.* Miami, FL: Academy of the Arts and Sciences of the Americas, 1973.

Graham, R. B. Cunninghame. *A Vanished Arcadia, Being Some Account of the Jesuits in Paraguay, 1607–1767.* London: William Heinemann, 1901.

Hennessy, Alistair. *The Frontier in Latin American History.* Albuquerque, NM: University of New Mexico Press, 1978.

Hopkins, Edward A., Raymond E. Crist, and William P. Snow. *Paraguay: 1852 and 1968*. Occasional Publication No. 2. New York: American Geographical Society, 1968.

Hudson, Peter. "'There Are No Terrorists Here': In a Lawless No Man's Land Deep in the Heart of South America, Muslims Face Down a Suspicious World." *Newsweek International*, Atlantic Edition (November 19, 2001): 39.

Lewis, Daniel K. *The History of Argentina*. New York: Palgrave, 2003.

Lewis, Paul H. *Paraguay Under Stroessner*. Chapel Hill, NC: University of North Carolina Press, 1980.

———. *Political Parties and Generations in Paraguay's Liberal Era, 1869–1940*. Chapel Hill, NC: University of North Carolina Press, 1993.

Library of Congress. *Terrorist and Organized Crime Groups in the Tri-border Area (TBA) of South America*. Washington, DC: Federal Research Division, Library of Congress, 2003.

———. *Transnational Activities of Chinese Crime Organizations*. Washington, DC: Federal Research Division, Library of Congress, 2003.

López, Adalberto. *The Revolt of the Comuñeros, 1721–1735: A Study in the Colonial History of Paraguay*. Cambridge, MA: Schenkman, 1976.

Lynch, John. *The Spanish American Revolutions 1808–1826*, 2nd ed. New York: W. W. Norton, 1986.

Moog, Vianna. *Bandeirantes and Pioneers*. New York: George Braziller, 1964.

N. A. "Free Trade with Brazil and Argentina Poses Threat to Smugglers in Ciudad del Este." *The Economist* (September 1, 1990): 62.

Nickson, R. Andrew. *Historical Dictionary of Paraguay*, 2nd ed. Metuchen, NJ: Scarecrow Press, 1993.

Rock, David. *Argentina, 1516–1982.* Berkeley: University of California Press, 1985.

Sciscioli, Alejandro. "Tension Over Presence of 'Brasiguayos'" Inter Press Service News Agency for Tierramérica Network. (November 21, 2003).

Service, Elman R. *Spanish-Guaraní Relations in Early Colonial Paraguay.* Westport, CT: Greenwood Press, 1971.

Simón, José Luis. "Drug Addiction and Trafficking In Paraguay: An Approach to the Problem During the Transition," *Journal of Interamerican Studies and World Affairs,* 34 (Autumn 1992), 3: 157–160.

Valente, Marcela. "South America: A Giant Valuable Aquifer and Rumors of Terrorists." Inter Press Service News Agency, February 18, 2004. http://www.factiva.com (October 14, 2004).

Vellinho, Moysés. *Brazil South: Its Conquest and Settlement.* New York: Alfred A. Knopf, 1968.

Whigham, Thomas. *The Paraguayan War: Causes and Early Conduct,* Vol. 1. Lincoln: University of Nebraska Press, 2002.

———. *The Politics of River Trade: Tradition and Development in the Upper Plata, 1780–1870.* Albuquerque: University of New Mexico Press, 1991.

Williams, John Hoyt. *The Rise and Fall of the Paraguayan Republic, 1800–1870.* Austin: University of Texas Press, 1979.

Wood, Randall. "Of Note: South America's Tri-border Region." *SAIS Review,* 25 (Winter–Spring 2005), 1: 105–106.

page:

ii: © Infobase Publishing
4: © Infobase Publishing
8: © Reuters/CORBIS
14: Associated Press, AP
17: © Ricardo Azoury/CORBIS
22: © Infobase Publishing
35: © Bojan Brecelj/CORBIS
42: © Infobase Publishing
48: © Infobase Publishing

59: © Getty Images
66: © Getty Images
76: © Bettmann/CORBIS
81: © Horacio Villalobos/CORBIS
84: © Bettmann/CORBIS
92: © Bettmann/CORBIS
96: Associated Press, AP
101: Associated Press, AP
107: © Reuters/CORBIS

Cover: © University of Texas at Austin

Daniel K. Lewis is Associate Professor and Chair of the History Department at California State Polytechnic University, Pomona. He is a specialist in Modern Latin America and California history. Author of *The History of Argentina*, he is currently researching the role of public agencies and private companies in the development of the Argentine grain farming industry before 1945.

George J. Mitchell served as chairman of the peace negotiations in Northern Ireland during the 1990s. Under his leadership, an historic accord, ending decades of conflict, was agreed to by the governments of Ireland and the United Kingdom and the political parties in Northern Ireland. In May 1998, the agreement was overwhelmingly endorsed by a referendum of the voters of Ireland, North and South. Senator Mitchell's leadership earned him worldwide praise and a Nobel Peace Prize nomination. He accepted his appointment to the U.S. Senate in 1980. After leaving the Senate, Senator Mitchell joined the Washington, D.C. law firm of Piper Rudnick, where he now practices law. Senator Mitchell's life and career have embodied a deep commitment to public service and he continues to be active in worldwide peace and disarmament efforts.

James I. Matray is Professor and Chair of the History Department at California State University, Chico. He has published more than forty articles and book chapters on U.S.–Korean relations during and after World War II. Author of *The Reluctant Crusade: American Foreign Policy in Korea, 1941–1950 and Japan's Emergence as a Global Power*, his most recent publication is *East Asia and the United States: An Encyclopledia of Relations Since 1784*. Matray also is international columnist for the *Donga Ilbo* in South Korea.